PORTFOLIO
THE JOY OF ACHIEVEMENT

Editor, publisher and author, Russi M. Lala began his career as a journalist in 1948, at the age of nineteen. Shortly after this, he became an executive in a book publishing house. In 1959, he became the manager of the first Indian book publishing house in London. In 1964, he founded (with Rajmohan Gandhi) the newsweekly, *Himmat*, which he edited for a decade.

In 1981 he published his first book *The Creation of Wealth: The Tata Story* to critical and commercial acclaim. This was followed by *Encounters with the Eminent* (1986), *The Heartbeat of a Trust* (1984) and *In Search of Leadership* (1986). He edited, with S.A. Sabavala, a book of J.R.D. Tata's speeches, *Keynote* (1986). His book *Beyond the Last Blue Mountain: A Life of J.R.D. Tata* (1992) was an immediate bestseller.

THE JOY
OF
ACHIEVEMENT

Conversations

with

JRD Tata

R. M. Lala

PORTFOLIO
PENGUIN

An imprint of Penguin Random House

PORTFOLIO

USA | Canada | UK | Ireland | Australia
New Zealand | India | South Africa | China | Singapore

Portfolio is part of the Penguin Random House group of companies
whose addresses can be found at global.penguinrandomhouse.com

Published by Penguin Random House India Pvt. Ltd
4th Floor, Capital Tower 1, MG Road,
Gurugram 122 002, Haryana, India

First published in Viking by Penguin Books India 1995
Published in Penguin Books 1997

18 17 16 15 14 13 12

ISBN 9780140250640

Typeset in Palatino by Digital Technologies and Printing Solutions, New Delhi
Printed at Manipal Technologies Limited, India

To the memory of
JEH and GOOL
in grateful remembrance
for the affection and the care
they bestowed on me

When thou wilt comfort and cheer thyself, call to mind the several gifts and virtues of them, whom thou dost daily converse with; as for example, the industry of the one; the modesty of another; the liberality of a third; of another some other thing. For nothing can so much rejoice thee, as the resemblances and parallels of several virtues, visible and eminent in the dispositions of those who live with thee; especially when, all at once, as near as may be, they represent themselves unto thee. And therefore thou must have them always in a readiness.

Marcus Aurelius
Meditations (Book 6 : XLIII)

'The business of the biographer is . . . . (to) display the minute details of daily life.'

Samuel Johnson
Rambler No. 60

CONTENTS

ACKNOWLEDGEMENTS

Two days after Mr J.R.D. Tata passed away, Mr. Xerxes Desai, Vice-Chairman and Managing Director of Titan Industries, wrote to me: 'I hope you will write again about the man who so dominated our lives and the Indian scene and reveal some more about his life, his personality, his hopes and his fears. Many of us have got to know him better through your books and we look to you to keep his memory alive.'

I am thankful to Mr Xerxes Desai for his letter which sparked off this book.

I am also thankful to:

My senior friend in England Mr Kenneth Belden, a publisher of vast experience, for going through the manuscript and for his suggestions.

Mr David Davidar of Viking/Penguin for his innovative ideas and his intense involvement in editing this book.

Mr Arvind Mambro, Principal Archival Officer, Tata Central Archives, for double-checking on historical facts.

Mr Sebastian Mathias for typing the drafts of the book and Mrs Villoo Karkaria for coordinating my work on this book.

Miss Khorshed A. Divecha and Miss Freny Shroff for their help in selecting the photographs and to Mr Jehangir Nicholson for sparing one of his personal snapshots of JRD.

PREFACE

A reader may well ask me: 'If you have already written the biography of J.R.D. Tata, where is the need for a second book on him?' The answer is quite simple. This book is not a substitute for the biography *Beyond the Last Blue Mountain*. Rather, it is supplementary to it. The biography was about the life and achievements of JRD. This book is about his thinking on various matters and about my encounters with him, especially in the two years after the biography was completed.

When I started the biography, I had a choice. I could have written a narrative that included a few details of his life and interspersed it with some anecdotes about him, some thoughts of his own. It would have perhaps been a shorter book than the four hundred page biography that was eventually published. The alternative choice was to write a standard biography covering his life and his achievements, a book that would be source material for future biographers, historians and readers—a biography that would do full justice to the achievements of one of the great Indians of this century.

The first option would have been easier to take. The second was a longer journey. I decided to go on the longer journey. I had access to all the material on JRD. In addition, my long association with and my knowledge of the House of Tatas as a result of writing *The Creation of Wealth* and editing, with S.A. Sabavala, a collection of JRD's speeches called *Keynote*, came in useful. I had also the privilege of ready access to my subject both as a biographer and as Director of the Sir Dorabji Tata Trust, of which JRD was the Chairman. Although it is a moot point now, even at the time when I was preparing to write *Beyond the Last Blue Mountain*, I knew it was unlikely that another biographer would have equal access to the person as well as to his papers. For all these reasons, I decided that a full-length biography was the book that would serve JRD best.

A standard biography is a structured book. It cannot be too cluttered with tittle-tattle as that would distract the reader from the essential thrust on what the subject of the biography achieved and how his personality developed. What does not fit into the essential structure has to be often omitted, even if reluctantly, or covered only briefly. In addition, the physical extent of the biography has to be kept in mind. I had to be conscious of the length both for the sake of the reader as well as of the subject of the biography. More than once JRD asked me, 'How many pages will your book be?'

I always replied: 'Four hundred pages.'

'How many pages is Frank Harris' book on J.N. Tata?'

'Three hundred and fifty pages.'

'Why should your biography of me be longer than that of J.N. Tata?'

'Because, J.N. Tata's active life spanned about thirty-five years and his was entirely a business life. Your active life is about twice that and covers both business and aviation.'

I reminded him that Frank Harris admitted in his book that he did not know J.N. Tata personally and said that it was because of this limitation that he did not call his book a biography of J.N. Tata, but merely a 'chronicle of his life'.

JRD was not convinced by my argument but accepted it anyway. In the event, when the first edition of *Beyond the*

Last Blue Mountain was published, by happy chance the book came to exactly four hundred pages.

Some reviewers of the biography noted that it was a remarkably 'self-effacing book' on the part of the author. Readers will pardon me if this book is not so 'self-effacing'. Most of these conversations did not appear in the biography and if mentioned were covered only briefly. The present book also deals with my interaction with him in the two years between the completion of the biography and his death. As Director of the Sir Dorabji Tata Trust and an advisor to the J.R.D. Tata Trust I dealt with him fairly often and kept note of my meetings. Some of these meetings gave me valuable insights into his personality, especially those occasions when he would say to me : 'Oh! Put these files aside, I like to talk to you.' He was often in a particularly expansive mood after 5.30 in the evenings and often have been the times when my wife, who came to collect me in the evenings, waited patiently—or impatiently—alone in my office, while I had the benefit of JRD's exhilarating company.

At this point I might venture to state that in my attempts to get to know the personality behind the public figure I had one advantage over his other colleagues. I had no association with any company and we seldom talked about business. He knew I wanted nothing but his friendship and he gave of that liberally. I, in turn, gave him mine. Most times he was great fun to be with. We both had a common interest in poetry. In the last years, especially when work was done and I would rise to go, he would switch on his mischief. One occasion comes to mind. Just before he went abroad for his angioplasty (heart procedure), I wished him good luck. As I turned to leave, he said plaintively, 'You know, at my age nobody is bothered what happens to me except myself.' There was a pause, and then he added in a louder tone, 'And the ladies!'

I turned to face him. 'Whose hearts you have broken?'

'No', he replied, smiling, 'whose favours I seek'.

A few months before he died, as I was walking towards the door after our interview, he said, 'Do you know why I like you so much, Russi?'

I looked back and enquired: 'Why?'

He smiled and said: 'Because we both are alike'.

As I turned again to leave, he added, 'We are both so w-e-a-k-minded'.

He was no saint. He had a glad eye for the ladies. He could relate very fine jokes and occasionally a naughty one. He once opened his personal red Tata diary and read out a joke that played on words and was rather derogatory to members of the British Labour Party of the 1940s. The arch conservative Winston Churchill said in his book *Great Contemporaries* that tittle-tattle can destroy a small man, but not a big man. And JRD was a big man. He was big in his vision, he was generous—sometimes over-generous—in his appreciation of people, and he was at the top of his job for sixty years. And throughout his long life he continued to grow in mind and spirit, even when his body weakened. He thought through the big issues of life and of the world he lived in. In a letter to Jayaprakash Narayan (JP) way back in 1955, he had predicted the demise of communism and that the communists would one day turn to a market economy. Again, he foresaw in a conversation with me, more than two years before the collapse of the Berlin Wall, that Russia would be very different in the near future. Perhaps the one area he was weak in, and he admitted as much to a respected theologian, Fr Balaguer, is that he had not read or thought enough about religion. Even a fortnight before he left India for good, he wanted to know about religion and we had a lengthy discussion quoted towards the end of this book.

I have chosen to divide this book into five parts. Part I, 'The Joy of Achievement', is a history of his life and is especially intended for those who have not read *Beyond the Last Blue Mountain*. Having said that, it should also be stressed that this section is written with the perspective gained by hindsight as well as the more recent perceptions of JRD, and for these reasons, even those who have read the biography may find it of some interest.

Part II, 'Conversations with JRD', is the heart of this book and presents his views on a variety of subjects, broadly divided into ten themes.

Part III, 'Fast Falls the Eventide' covers the last four years of his life.

Part IV, 'Glimpses into a Crucial Year—1991', comprises notes I kept during what was in many ways a crucial year in JRD's life.

Part V, 'The Last Year', is about key events in his life in the year in which he died.

In the Appendix I've included JRD's Foreword from his book of speeches *Keynote*. Also as an Appendix I've included a personal account of the story behind the writing of *Beyond the Last Blue Mountain*, my biography of JRD Tata. This answers the question I'm sometimes asked about how I interacted with him as his biographer. A third Appendix is the hymn 'Abide with Me', on which there was a discussion with him. The hymn was played at his funeral.

I should add at this point that JRD was almost fanatical about getting his sentences and language right whenever he chose to express himself. As this book was put together after his death, I have taken the liberty of slightly editing recorded interviews with him in order to fulfil the requirements of grammar and syntax; this editing has been kept to a minimum. Unlike his written word about which he was so particular, it is good to remember that when he spoke he was very relaxed and did not feel under the same obligation.

Weeks after his death, articles, letters, advertisements and hoardings about him continued to appear. The message from his former company, Air India, would have pleased him immensely:

> *He touched the sky
> and it smiled.
> He stretched out his arms
> and they encircled the globe.
> His vision made giants out of
> men and organizations.*

Another hoarding said in large white letters on a black ground: 'The Spirit of JRD lives on'.

I hope this book will enable the spirit of a vibrant, charming visionary to live on.

R. M. Lala
Bombay 1 March 1995

I

THE JOY OF ACHIEVEMENT

Dreams

Hold fast to dreams
For if dreams die
Life is a broken-winged bird
That cannot fly.

Hold fast to dreams
For when dreams go
Life is a barren field
Frozen with snow

Langston Hughes

Sketch by. J. R. D. Tata

By the same author

THE JOY OF ACHIEVEMENT

Despite all the difficulties, all the frustrations, there is a joy in having done something as well as you could and better than others thought you could.

> —J.R.D. Tata, on the 50th Anniversary flight of his launching civil aviation in India.

The life of JRD (1904-93) spanned almost the whole of the twentieth century. He was born in Paris and he died in Geneva. In between, he spent over seventy years of his working life in India. During that period, he brought to India the gift of civil aviation in 1932 and later, in 1948, helped the country spread her wings abroad by launching Air India International. Thirty years later, when he was removed as Chairman of Air India, the *Daily Telegraph* (27 February 1978) of London, among others, credited him with making Air India 'one of the world's most successful airlines'. Had he achieved nothing else his place in India's hall of fame would still have been secure; but he did far more.

For fifty-two years he was Chairman of the largest industrial group in India—Tata—which produced everything from steel and electric power to chemicals and automobiles. Apart from Air-India (which was nationalized), Tata Chemicals and TELCO, both started under his Chairmanship, became two of India's top ten companies in both sales and assets.

On the social scene, he was the first national voice to call for family planning. Prime Minister Jawaharlal Nehru disagreed with him and said that the country's strength was its people. Undeterred, for forty years he pursued a campaign to promote family planning, especially through the agency he founded—the Family Planning Association of India. Belated recognition came to him for this effort: the last of the many international awards he received was the U.N. Population Award. Two national institutions—the Tata Institute of Fundamental Research and the National Centre for the Performing Arts, which we shall look at in some detail later on—were started because of his support and vision. A third, the National Institute of Advanced Studies, was inaugurated by him two years before he died.

For thirty years, JRD raised his voice against the misguided policies of a controlled economy that stunted the country's industrial growth and destroyed his own dreams for India's industrial future. Once when I entered his office, even before I could sit down, he said, 'You know, Russi, my life has been a struggle—never once has any Prime Minister asked me what I thought of the economic policy of the country.' Sadly, he added, 'In no other country would this have happened.'

Nevertheless, undaunted, he articulated his convictions whenever it was appropriate. He said: 'I felt that if my small voice in the national economic debate could arouse public opinion, it was my duty to use it to oppose the outdated and sterile form of socialism which successive governments insisted on inflicting on the country year after year despite all the contrary evidence and experience in India and elsewhere in the world.' It was only after three decades that he could perceive a chink in the government's rusted armour of socialism and controls. Speaking at the age of eighty-two at the launch of *Keynote* in Delhi in 1986, he said: 'My one sorrow and regret is that the Government had, from Jawaharlal Nehru onwards, and at least upto a couple of years ago, not allowed many of us imbued with enthusiasm and hope to do enough. Today things have changed and now the last sorrow of mine is that I have reached an age where I am not likely to be able to participate purposefully in the better things that are happening, the better progress and the quicker progress that I visualize.' He concluded : 'I only wish that I'll be spared long enough to see that we are on the march.'

He was spared long enough to hear five years later the budget speech of July 1991 by the Finance Minister Manmohan Singh, which liberated India's economy from the shackles of the past. Soon after the budget speech, I remarked that it must have been gratifying to see what he had battled for at last being accepted by the Government. He took no credit; he felt that the bankruptcy of the Government's policies had made them take a U-turn and that his unflagging battle had had little to do with the new thinking and policy.

The one thing that everyone who knew him remarked upon was the manner in which he prevailed over the setbacks and disappointments that he encountered in the course of the numerous activities and initiatives he concerned himself with. The frustrations and reversals, which would have exhausted a lesser man, appeared only to exhilarate him. It was so because he fought without malice. For example, though he disagreed with Nehru on economic policy, he still had a great personal affection for him. He could distinguish between the public stance of a man and his private virtues and friendship. Though often distressed at the way the country was going, his spirit remained buoyant until almost the last hundred days of his life because he found fulfilment in creative achievement, and he continued to achieve where others might have faltered.

He once told me, 'I've made sure that I don't have much money.' In 1944, when he was only forty years old, he gave part of his wealth to the JRD Tata Trust, which had disbursed well over ten million rupees to charity in his lifetime. Every penny of the Trust came from him. Money was never the driving force of his life. What propelled him was the joy of achievement. Let me illustrate this. He undertook two flights to commemorate the thirtieth and fiftieth anniversary of his launching of civil aviation in India. Few people would have attempted the first flight, but to do the second was nothing short of extraordinary. For, in 1982, when he 're-enacted' the fiftieth anniversary flight from Karachi to Bombay in a single-engine Leopard Moth, he was seventy-eight years old. On landing he told the crowd that had assembled to greet him, 'This flight of mine today was intended to inspire a little hope and enthusiasm in the younger people of our country. I hope they all will live at least to seventy-eight— they will feel like I do, that despite all the difficulties, all the frustrations, there is a joy in having done something as well as you could and better than others thought you could.'

Unusually, his joy lay not only in what he personally achieved, but also in the achievement of the other individuals whom he had groomed and who worked for him. When he stepped down after fifty-two years as Chairman of Tata Sons, the press noted that he was the only eminent industrialist in the country who had nurtured, within his own organisation, people who had grown into corporate giants in their own right.

As we've seen earlier , JRD's joy of achievement extended beyond the ambit of business to the institutions he helped create. Significant among them was the Tata Institute of Fundamental Research (T.I.F.R.), where he stood beside Dr Homi Bhabha as Bhabha shaped 'the cradle of India's atomic energy programme'. His belief that without art and music man is incomplete, resulted in his support to Homi's brother Jamshed Bhabha for the creation of the National Centre for the Performing Arts. In addition to these two was the part he played in the foundation of the National Institute of Advanced Studies in Bangalore.

He also had a decisive role in the planning stage of India's first (and still the foremost) cancer hospital—Tata Memorial. There was a debate as to the scale and extent of the proposed hospital, given the then limited funds of the Trust. The minutes of the meeting of the Sir Dorabji Tata Trust (13 November 1937) show that it was J.R.D. Tata who, as a trustee, was particular that it should not have only radium treatment and surgery, but that 'this hospital should be able to carry out the triple objectives of treatment, research and education. We should treat research almost as important as treatment.' It has taken some years but today the Cancer Research Institute stands next to the Tata Memorial Hospital.

In 1939, when Dr Homi Bhabha had come to Bombay from Cambridge for a holiday and could not return because of disruption caused by World War II, he was given an alternative career option by J.R.D. Tata, who arranged to have a special Cosmic Ray unit opened at the Indian Institute of Science, Bangalore, so that this brilliant young scientist could continue his work without hindrance. Four years later, on 19 August 1943, Dr Homi Bhabha wrote to JRD that the lack of proper conditions and intelligent financial support were hampering the development of science in India. Scientific talent, he argued, was withering for lack of nourishment. He cited his own example and said that despite the allure of jobs abroad, in his view it was one's duty to stay in one's own country and help build its scientific infrastructure; however, for this it was imperative that funds were made available. JRD replied:

> If you and/or some of your colleagues in the scientific world will put up concrete proposals backed by a sound case, I think there is a very good chance that the Sir Dorab Tata Trust . . . will respond. After all, the advancement of science is one of the fundamental objectives with which most of the Tata Trusts were founded, and they have already rendered useful service in that field. If they are shown that they can give still more valuable help in a new way, I am quite sure that they will give it their most serious consideration.

Dr Homi Bhabha had foreseen the then little-known prospect of harnessing the energy of the atom for generating electric power. A year later he wrote to the Trust of his plans. The issue was debated by the trustees on 14 April 1945. The discussion centred around whether a poor country like India could afford the luxury of pure research when there were such pressing economic problems before it. The Trust accepted J.R.D. Tata's view that fundamental research was necessary. Three months later, with the bombing of Hiroshima, the world realized the power of nuclear energy. Six weeks prior to the nuclear explosion, J.R.D. Tata tried to interest a wealthy industrialist friend to support the project along with the Tata Trust. In a letter to him dated 22 June 1945, JRD spelt out his vision of what this institute could do for the country:

'I sincerely believe that this Institute can make a great contribution to the scientific knowledge of mankind . . . . You may perhaps feel that advanced physics, mathematics, astrophysics, are particularly abstract subjects, research in which is unlikely to produce material or practical results within a reasonable period of time. I should, however, like to point out that most of the great practical advances in science, and, therefore, in industry, have had their origins in fundamental research, without which they would have been impossible or would have been long delayed.

'Although nuclear physics is today still in the realm of pure science, physicists already believe that within a relatively short period of time, this branch of physics will make available to man a new, immense, and inexhaustible source of motive power. Thanks to the work done in this field by Bhabha and some other Indian scientists, India has already contributed her full share to the present day knowledge of the subject. More than ever before, the future of modern civilization will depend on scientific progress and that progress itself will continue to depend on pure research. Because the realization of this is becoming universal, all the important countries of the world have enormously increased the extent and scope of their activities in pure research, and India should not be allowed to lag behind in this vital quest for knowledge. She has men of world renown like Homi Bhabha, Chandrashekhar and others, and given proper facilities she is more than capable of holding her own.'

No doubt for reasons of his own, JRD's industrialist friend did not respond. But the then Government of Bombay and the Government of India did. Years later, speaking of the T.I.F.R., Dr Homi Bhabha said it was 'the cradle of India's atomic energy programme'.

The Institute built the first nuclear reactor in India, Apsara, in a wartime hutment. It was an achievement which put India in the forefront of atomic energy capabilities where the developing world was concerned. Over forty-six scientists went from the T.I.F.R. to what is now called the Bhabha Atomic Research Centre, formerly the Atomic Energy Training School started in 1957. The scientists included Dr Raja Ramanna. Dr Bhabha stated, 'If the Atomic Energy Establishment at Trombay has been able to develop so fast, it is due to the assisted take-off which was given to it by the Institute in the early stages of its development. It is equally true to say that the Institute could not have developed to its present size and importance but for the support it has received from the Government of India.' Dr Homi Bhabha's successor, Prof. M.G.K. Menon, wrote to J.R.D. Tata years later (5 April 1970): 'This institute would have never been what it is today but for the support you gave Homi to set it up and the continuing support you have given it ever since.'

JRD not only assisted the initial take-off, he gave of himself to the Institute. For example, the then Registrar of the T.I.F.R., N.R. Puthran, remembers JRD accompanying Dr. Homi Bhabha on Sunday mornings to supervise the building of even the theatre at the Institute at Colaba. JRD gave his friendship to Homi Bhabha, whom he described as one of the most versatile men he had met in his life.

On a visit to France in the 1960s, JRD was intrigued by the fact that seventy-five per cent of the top bureaucrats

and bankers of France were educated at one of the four
Grande L'Ecole Polytechniques of France—the first of which
was established by Napoleon to train civil engineers. JRD
invited Jean Capelle, Director General of Education, Paris,
to go round India with a group of educationists from within
the country in order to report whether a similar situation
could work in India. He wanted to submit such a proposal
to the Nehru Memorial Trust, for which he had already
raised a substantial sum of money. Unfortunately, nothing
came of the proposal at the time. Eighteen years later, after
stepping down from the Chairmanship of TISCO, at the
age of eighty he took up a project that he was unable to
execute at the age of sixty-two. The second time round he
was open to having the whole issue looked at afresh, because
unlike in 1966, by the mid 1980s the Indian Institutes of
Technology (IITs) and the Indian Institutes of Management
(IIMs) had established themselves as first-rate institutions
and the needs of the country were obviously different now.
He put together a Working Group consisting of people like
Dr L.K. Jha, Dr H.N. Sethna and Prof. Rustum Choksi, and
for advice he looked to Prof. P. Olmer, former Director of
Higher Education, Ministry of Education, Paris, who was
well acquainted with the Grande L'Ecole Polytechnique of
France. On their recommendation the National Institute of
Advanced Studies was set up in Bangalore with Dr Raja
Ramanna as the first Director.

When Homi Bhabha's brother Jamshed Bhabha
approached his fellow-Trustees at the Sir Dorabji Tata Trust
to start a National Centre for the Performing Arts (NCPA),
one of the senior Trustees tried to make light of it, saying
that now the Trust money was going into creating facilities
for ladies to perform the Bharat Natyam. Once again JRD
strongly supported the project. 'While we want to build a

prosperous society, we do not want to be merely a materialistic consumer society,' he stated.

Laying the foundation stone for the Tata Theatre at the NCPA in Bombay, JRD explained, ' We turned to the field of arts, already having covered medical relief, science and education, because we felt that there was a special need for it in this country where the great classical heritage in drama, music and dancing, what you call the performing arts, is gradually in the process of disappearing. Whereas in other countries of the world these arts are recorded either in writing—or these days on tape or record—and of course the plastic arts, the non-performing arts, are all recorded in stone, paintings, etc., Indian art and music, dancing and drama were not recorded and were passed on from guru to shishya, master to pupil. With the gradual erosion of the classical tradition, the work of the masters that was still alive was gradually dying out. The first task of the National Centre was to preserve and record the heritage, such of it as is available today, and the second task, of course, was to promote, as far as possible, a renaissance of Indian dramatic arts, the performing arts as we call them.'

JRD was also the first leading industrialist to recognize the responsibilities of business towards rural uplift. Speaking at a meeting at Madras in 1969 he said : 'Let industry established in the countryside "adopt" the villages in its neighbourhood; let some of the time of its managers, its engineers, doctors and skilled specialists be spared to help and advise the people of the villages and to supervise new developments undertaken by co-operative effort between them and the company. Assistance in family planning in the villages would be a particularly valuable form of service. None or little of this need be considered as charity . . . . The benefits of such a joint venture will no doubt initially flow chiefly to the village, but it is also clearly in the interests of industry that surrounding areas should be healthy, prosperous and peaceful.'

To put JRD's ideas into action, the Articles of Association of leading Tata Companies were amended and social obligations beyond the welfare of their own employees were accepted as part of the objectives of the companies in question.

Clearly, JRD was interested in other people rather than in his own self. This applied not only to people he was acquainted with but even to people he did not know. When he heard about a young employee in one of the Tata companies who was having trouble deciding whether to emigrate or not, he called him to his office and said: 'Why didn't you talk to me? Why don't you use me while I am still here?'

For those he didn't know, he had a smile. 'The trouble is,' he would say, 'we don't smile enough. When I am driving in the car, and a person appears to recognize me, I look at that person and smile. This makes him happy and does not cost me anything.' He snatched joy from the little moments of life we often let pass in our preoccupation with ourselves. And the fact that his joy was selfless, in that he wanted others to feel joyful as well, is amply illustrated by the following example.

Hearing that an American economist had noted that India could be an 'economic super power' in the next century, JRD told an audience simply: 'I don't want India to be an economic super power. I want India to be a happy country.'

Whatever he touched, he adorned. His mother tongue was French; he loved the language and was good at it. When he settled in India in his early twenties, he decided that he would master the English language, and this he did. And he never relaxed in this endeavour. Until the very end, he took endless trouble to select the exact words he needed to express his thoughts. When he took to flying, he read almost all the books he could get hold of on aviation in the 1920s. When he began to play golf, he read books on golf. When he decided to learn tennis and bridge, he studied material on the two games. JRD never did things by halves, but always wanted to excel. As his long-standing secretary Raymond D'Souza said, 'He had to be in the driver's seat.' And although it was not in his nature to drive people he worked with, he did expect the best of them. An official of Air-India was once woken up at midnight about an Air India hoarding which JRD did not like. Recalling the incident the official said he could not find it in himself to object to the midnight call because 'JRD gave so much of himself'.

He was one of those whose love for India was kindled during the freedom struggle. He first met Jawaharlal Nehru, a man he hero-worshipped when he was younger, in 1924 when Motilal Nehru stayed with R.D. Tata in Bombay. As his friendship with and his admiration for Nehru and his colleagues grew, for a brief spell in 1942 JRD was tempted to participate actively in the freedom struggle. But he held himself back. His role was to forge the economic independence of India.

He recalls that at Independence, when he was forty-three, he was much enthused. 'I had tremendous dreams and expectations of cooperation between the private sector and the Government.' But his dreams did not come true, except with Air India International in 1948.

Nevertheless, he persevered in his pursuit of this initiative. Writing in *Current Science* Prof. Satish Dhawan

recalls JRD's visit to Bangalore: 'Sometime in 1992 he
enquired from a small group of people in Bangalore what
India should be doing in aerospace. He listened very
attentively to suggestions that the establishment of an
Indian aerospace industry quite outside of HAL and the
defence-controlled plants was long overdue and entirely
feasible. Long a supporter of private initiative it is a measure
of his wisdom when he remarked that the most likely success
would be for a mixed private-public industrial manufac-
turing enterprise—not only of aircraft but also the
accessories and the ground handling equipment related to
extended civil aerial operations.' There was always a certain
consistency to JRD's thinking that the government and the
private sector work hand in hand.

● ● ●

J.R.D. Tata was a product of two continents. His father,
R.D. (Ratanji Dadabhoy) Tata, was a cousin and colleague
of Jamsetji Tata, the man who brought the industrial
revolution to India, giving it steel, hydro-electric power and
high level technological education. In time, when he was
in his early forties, R.D. Tata decided to start his own
business in Paris, dealing in precious stones. Once in France,
he began taking tuitions in French from a Madame Briere.
In time he fell in love with Madame Briere's daughter and
proposed. They were married in 1902. She was twenty and
he was forty-two. Their marriage created a sensation
because R.D. Tata had not only married outside his Parsi
community but had also taken the revolutionary step of
having his European and Christian wife converted to the
Zoroastrian faith. Suzanne Briere changed her name to
Sooni.

Born in Paris in 1904, JRD schooled in Paris, Bombay and Yokohama. He also attended an English crammer school briefly, in order to improve his English. It was not until he was twenty-one that he settled down in India.

According to JRD, his mother was a very resourceful, intelligent and adaptable lady, who—first with two, then three, four and five children—singlehandedly packed up her household in France and came to India to be with her husband who had rejoined the House of Tatas. As she went back to her home country every year or two, JRD's education was regularly disrupted. His grandmother was a very formidable lady. Her husband was a humorist and after some time with her, says JRD, the gentleman 'ran away as anyone would have, had he been married to my grandmother.' Perhaps JRD inherited his sense of humour from his French grandfather.

Bleriot, the first man to fly across the English Channel, had a house on the coast of France near R.D. Tata's house. Bleriot's pilot, who used to land a small plane on the beach nearby, once gave JRD a joy ride. It was then that the fifteen-year-old boy decided that one day he too would fly. He had to wait ten years for it to happen.

After school he was drafted for a year into the French Army and assigned to a regiment in France called *Le Saphis*. At the end of his year, he intended to continue to serve with his regiment for a further six months and then go on to Cambridge where a place was reserved for him. But his father summoned him back to India.

It is just as well that R.D. Tata refused JRD an extension in the army. Soon after JRD left for India, the regiment was transferred to Morocco and in a battle they were killed to the last man. But till the end of his life the fact that he was not sent to Cambridge rattled JRD. He said it gave him 'an inferiority complex'.

Upon returning to India, JRD was inducted into the House of Tatas for training in 1925. About nine months later, in 1926, his father died and he became a director of the largest industrial house of India, whose interests ranged from steel and electric power to soap and textiles.

'Because of a lack of technical knowledge, my main contribution in management was to encourage others,' he said in an interview. He elaborated on how he dealt with each man in his own way and brought out the best in people. 'At times it involved suppressing yourself. It is painful but necessary.' He added, 'To lead men, you have to lead them with affection.'

In 1929, JRD passed out of flying school with No. 1 on his licence. He was the first Indian pilot. A year later he competed for the Aga Khan Trophy. It was offered for the first Indian to fly solo from India to England or vice versa. When he landed at Aboukir Bay in Egypt, he found that Aspy Engineer, the other contender, who was flying from London to Karachi, was stranded for want of a spark plug. JRD sportingly parted with his spare one and they continued their journey in opposite directions. Aspy beat him by a couple of hours. 'I am glad he won,' said JRD, 'because it helped him get into the Indian Air Force.' Later, Aspy was to be the second Indian to be Chief of the Indian Air Force.

JRD was to have a few other adventures. In the early 1930s, a daring Englishman called Nevill Vintcent came to India and travelled the country offering joy rides in a small plane. He suggested to JRD that they start an airline. That was JRD's dream, too, but Sir Dorabji Tata, then Chairman of the House of Tatas, was not interested. Finally, JRD's mentor, a retired I.C.S. official called John Peterson, persuaded Sir Dorab to agree and Tata Airlines was launched as a division of Tata Sons.

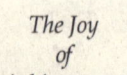
'One October morning as the sun rose on the eastern horizon, a single-engined Pussmoth plane took off from Karachi with a load of mail for Bombay. As the plane hummed and rose the pilot said a word of prayer,' recalled JRD, who was at the controls that day. And so India's first airline was inaugurated. Aeroplanes were looked upon as a rich man's luxury at the time, but as he flew these slow tiny planes with their mail, JRD had a vision that the future belonged to aviation which would knit together a country as large as India.

When asked whether he had done any stunt flying, he said he had and had once been within ten seconds of disaster. The only thing that had saved him was the fact that he had been cautious enough to go up to six thousand feet before he started descending. 'My instructor,' he said, 'did a criminal thing in releasing me to fly solo without teaching me how to get into and out of a spin. Fortunately I had read about it. When you are in a fast spin with full engines and you want to pull out, your temptation is to draw the joy stick (to yourself) and then even off. This can prove fatal.' Fortunately for him, after he had dived from six thousand to one thousand feet, he remembered what he had read. Accordingly, he centred the joy stick, and, to his relief, the plane evened off. When he landed JRD was furious with his instructor for releasing him to fly solo without essential instructions. 'To be a safe pilot you must know how to spin,' said JRD.

The airline he pioneered later blossomed into Air India International and in 1948, in a joint venture with the Indian Government, JRD launched Air India's first overseas route to London. In the beginning Air India's office was housed in a caravan at the airport in London.Over the next thirty years, under JRD's constant care, it grew into one of the world's finest airlines. Throughout that period he spent about half of his day working for Air India and the other half for the vast industrial enterprises of Tatas. To Air India he gave his services as a labour of love and took no remuneration.

With more than sixty years of experience in top management, he developed his own philosophy and method where leadership was concerned. 'One of the qualities of leadership is to assess what is needed to get the best results for an enterprise. If that demands being a very active executive chairman as I was in Air India, I did that. On the other hand, in one of our other companies where I know that the managing director likes to be alone and will get the results that way, I argue with myself and decide that it will be stupid for me to come in the way when the other person has a capacity for focussing his genius and producing the results. Often a chairman's main responsibility is to inspire respect.' And then he added, 'Don't forget, I like people.'

● ● ●

When JRD was thirty-four, the then Chairman of Tatas died suddenly. Three of the senior directors met and elected young JRD to be Chairman of the parent company, Tata Sons. When I asked him why they elected him at such a young age, he replied modestly: 'It was a case of mental aberration.' It was usual for the Tata Chairman to head all the Tata companies. JRD discontinued that practice and kept in his charge only those companies where he felt his presence was essential.

Six months after JRD took over as Chairman of Tata Sons, the company launched Tata Chemicals on 1 January 1939 at Mithapur. In the first sixteen years the company could

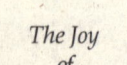
pay a dividend only once and Tata Sons carried the company throughout this period. An international expert invited by Tata's advised JRD: 'You are in the wrong place doing the wrong job.' Undaunted, he replied: 'This is not the first time we have done this.' He added that 'when we go to a place (Mithapur) we arouse the hopes in people.' For their sake, as much as for any other reason, Mithapur had to succeed. He was always proud that at that crucial point he discovered within Tata Chemicals a thirty-one-year-old chemical engineer called Darbari Seth who was being held back by his superiors, and he gave this young man a free hand. Tata Chemicals was turned around and is today one of the group's most prosperous companies. JRD had a very high threshold of endurance and believed in holding a decision until he was clear rather than rushing it—except when an urgent decision was needed.

When asked: 'What has been the most satisfying experience of your life?' JRD replied: 'The flying experience has dominated and no other can equal the excitement of the first solo flight. Next is Air India, where I had the freedom to do what I wanted. In a way it was the really big thing that I started.' He was being modest. It was he who started TELCO which reached staggering heights and now commands seventy per cent of the heavy vehicle market in India. Other Tata companies that he was especially close to were Tata Sons and Tata Steel where he began his career.

JRD sought satisfaction in many other ways. All his life he was keen on physical fitness and he took the trouble to exercise until 1987. His motivation was to keep fit for skiing till he fell off a ski cable car—'a stupid accident' he called it—and suffered a hairline fracture. He played tennis and especially golf till his mid-seventies. He was proud he took up skiing at forty, an age when people normally retire from

the sport, and continued to ski until he was eighty-four
years old. As a young man he loved fast cars and drove
round Bombay in his Bugatti which was a racing model
without mudguards. If aviation had not claimed him, it is
likely he might have contemplated competing in Grand Prix
events. When he was in his early eighties he wrote in
Keynote: 'Friends who tell me it is ridiculous and foolhardy
for an octogenarian to ski, fly a plane or drive fast cars, do
not understand the thrill and sense of self-fulfilment obtained
from living a little dangerously.'

Despite his ability to keep himself engaged, nothing
dulled JRD's sensitivity to human suffering and to the
subhuman conditions in which many of his fellow citizens
existed. Once, when he saw a poor man crossing a road in
Bombay, he said to me, 'Look at that poor man carrying
probably all his belongings on his head.'

He yearned to be a fountain of living water to those less
fortunate than himself and this was reflected in the scale
and extent of his philanthropic activities. Among other
concerns, he felt deeply about the condition of women in
India and a couple of years before he died he established a
Trust of his own called the J.R.D. and Thelma J. Tata Trust
to ameliorate the condition of women.

Rewards, decorations and other forms of recognition
were not something he craved for, yet his work in every
field he involved himself in was so exemplary that the
honours poured in. He was the recipient of the Daniel
Guggenheim Award and some of the highest awards in
aviation like the Tony Janus Award. And, in 1992, the Bharat
Ratna, his country's highest civilian decoration, was
bestowed upon him. After the Bharat Ratna, when I
observed that God had preserved him till the last decade of
the century to be the recipient of this award, which came
after many others, he replied: 'No more! No more!'

When BBC TV announced his death in Geneva on 29 November 1993, it called JRD 'the legendary Indian industrialist'. Yet, for all his worldly power and glory, to those who knew him he was a warm-hearted, caring human being. 'I want to be remembered,' he had said, 'as an honest man who did his duty.'

II

CONVERSATIONS

with J.R.D. Tata

EARLY YEARS

FIRST CHILDHOOD RECOLLECTION

On 29 July 1904, JRD was born in Paris. He was named Jehangir, 'Conqueror of the World'.

JRD : My recollections of very early babyhood days are nil. But I remember when I was about four, must have been 1908, I got a thrashing from my father for having kicked the ayah.

RML : That is one of your first recollections?

JRD : Yes, and when she remonstrated with me I said, 'I can hit you, kick you because you're poor.' Can you imagine (me doing it)? So when she repeated it to my mother and my mother told my father, my father quite rightly gave me a thrashing. Never understood how anybody could ever say something like that.

● ● ●

JRD said he did not know his father too well as he had seen so little of him. He knew his mother better and spoke glowingly about her. She was stunningly good-looking with blue eyes and golden hair and once he mentioned how when he 'entered a restaurant with (his) mother, everybody turned to look at her and I was jealous'. His mother died when he was only eighteen.

JRD's sister, Rodabeh Sawhny, adds: 'Mother was so interested in everything, very beautiful in a way that was very colourful. She had golden hair and a tinge of blue in her eyes that I've searched for in others. She was a very accomplished lady. Within six months of coming to India she had learnt Gujarati and could write to her husband in Gujarati. She spent a lot of the time away from India due to ill health towards the end of her life but wrote daily to her husband. She could tailor clothes and make hats; her pastry was out of this world and so was her cooking. She had a sparkling personality, very witty and alert. We had a very happy childhood. Travelled a lot—came to Bombay; went to France; spent two years in Japan.'

● ● ●

FATHER

JRD : My father had no money at all. In fact he lived in Navsari. My father used to tell me that until he was about fifteen or eighteen and came to Bombay, he used to walk barefoot in Navsari. Was of a humble family and yet I don't know how Jamsetji Tata picked him up because Jamsetji Tata made him an associate member[*] right from the start.

Rodabeh recalls that after their mother died in 1923, the children came to India. R.D. used to come back early from office about 4.30, because he wanted to be with the children, especially the younger three. R.D. was a great one for physical exercises and he used to do all his exercises and get the children to exercise with him. He smoked, but not much. Meanwhile the house, 'Sunita' (named after and built for his wife Sooni), was decorated with everything French—not only the furniture, but to the last details of locks and handles.

He did pray at nights on the verandah facing the Chowpatty sea but he wore no cap.

When R.D. died friends told the children that 'he had the heart of a lion'.

● ● ●

THE DEATH OF HIS PARENTS

JRD's mother lay seriously ill in Paris in 1923. His father was in Bombay, fighting for the survival of Tata Steel, and could not leave Bombay to see her. Finally, the day he stepped on board a P & O liner to go and see her, he received news that she had died. He spent just a week in France with his children, settled affairs and sailed again for India.

---

[*] Partner of Tata and Sons, Jamsetji's original company founded in 1887.

R.D. Tata and Sir Dorabji Tata, who pledged his entire fortune for a loan from the Imperial Bank, steered Tata Steel out of the precarious situation. Soon after, JRD was due to enter Cambridge when his father called him to India. JRD returned in late 1925, and his father sent him to Jamshedpur for training within a few months of his arrival. R.D. left for France in the summer of 1926. He died there in August and was buried beside his wife in Paris.

Jeh was only twenty-two and he became the head of the family. He had no uncles or close relatives to help or advise him, save a reliable friend and solicitor called Dinshaw Daji of Crawford Bailey & Co.

● ● ●

HIS SISTER ON JRD

I asked JRD's sister, Mrs Rodabeh Sawhny, 'What fault would you pick in Jeh if you had to pick one?'

Mrs Sawhny thought for a long time then said: 'Impatience. He is human. He is impatient, especially with his family.'

She pondered a little longer. 'He has not allowed his family in any way to intrude on his work. He would tell us, "I have not got time." He is less busy now. He has not given preference to his family. For example, Nusli Petit, Sylla's son, was on his own in Europe in Air India and later joined a company in Holland.

● ● ●

RML : Have you any memories of your father's reactions to the boorish behaviour of some Parsis towards your mother when she had her *Navjote* (her induction into the Zoroastrian faith)?

JRD : My recollection is very dim on that. From what I have read later and from talks with my father, my impression is that she was not treated boorishly. They objected to having this foreign woman inducted into the Zoroastrian faith with the *Navjote* (thread ceremony).

I once asked JRD if his own attitude to Parsis was coloured by members of the community objecting to his mother's *Navjote* and wedding according to Parsi rites. Promptly he replied, 'I don't think so.'

About his own *Navjote*, JRD said it took place not in their home but at 'some public place'. He remembered that when a small glass of *Taraa* (white bull's urine with disinfectant qualities to be sipped at the *Navjote* ceremony) was offered to him, his mother swooped down on it and threw it away.

● ● ●

EDUCATION

JRD's education was disrupted time and again. He schooled in Paris with French as the medium of instruction for a couple of years, then in Bombay in English, then Paris again, before returning to Bombay once more. In between, he even spent about two years in Japan.

RML : Do you remember anything at all about your time at Cathedral High School in Bombay?

JRD : None at all. I've no recollection. Frankly, during my stay at Cathedral, which was only on two occasions for a year each, I was bored stiff with the way I was taught. They didn't even teach you proper English! I enjoyed mathematics, physics, whatever was taught . But I don't know why I was bored by British history. I used to say, '(But) What has happened in India?' The only thing they would never teach you anything about was India. I seem to have a very good recollection of being smacked down once for asking, 'What about Aurangzeb?' I don't know why I said Aurangzeb.

After Cathedral, school in England, and a year with a French regiment, he was, as we've seen, unable to get to Cambridge as planned and instead returned to India as instructed by his father, who died a few months later in 1926.

'My father should have sent me to school in England,' said JRD, 'knowing one day I would come out to India and work here. But he was so fond of France and of mother that he sent me back to France in 1919, useless from the point of my future career. Maybe Father did not realize that while a university education is not necessary , it is important.'

As this unresolved regret kept coming up in conversations with him, I remarked that had he been to Cambridge he may not have had the same bright future in

---

* His own command of English at that time was very limited and he

Tatas that he finally had. He seemed to agree but even so it rankled him that he had not been to a University and not been able to specialize in any field. It was this deprivation, if one may call it that, which made him determined to excel in whatever he did, and the number of things he was good at is amazing. Apart from business, he was good at metalwork, his English was excellent, he was a fine editor, he knew quite a lot of poetry, both English and French. He read a good deal of history and could often assess events with remarkable insight.

●　　●　　●

'I WANT TO BE WORTHY OF TATAS'

Talking of JRD's first years at Tatas, his sister, Mrs Rodabeh Sawhny, said, 'Jeh used to stay at the Taj after 'Sunita' was sold. At twenty-two he had typhoid and soon after, two attacks of para typhoid. He was extremely thin and he had fever most nights. He used to come to his room at the Taj dead beat from the office, throw himself on his bed and then start studying books on business and management— "to make myself worthy of Tatas," he would say. He knew he would become Chairman one day. Jeh had always hoped to go to Oxford or Cambridge but he could not, and so he sharpened his mind and trained himself. He made himself. If Jeh is what he is today it was not because he was my father's son. It is due to him. He cured himself of his ill health by a milk cure. For some time he drank nothing but milk the whole day, and later took to physical culture.

I asked JRD if his sister's picture of this period in his life was accurate.

32

The Joy
of
Achievement

JRD : I had typhoid a number of times when young, para typhoid two-three times.

RML : You can have typhoid more than once?

JRD : No, but I got para typhoid and then I also had amoebic dysentery.

RML : And you came home after a hard day's work and often studied books on economics and management on your own.

JRD : No. I won't exaggerate. I read a lot but not so much books as articles or magazines. Technical magazines, foreign magazines. No, I can't claim that (studying books).

RML : Did you have a private tutor to teach you?

JRD : Yes, only to try and teach me Hindi, but it turned out to be Urdu. He used to come to the office. I'm going to start that again now, if I can find a man who can teach me Hindustani and not Hindi. But then I got one who was a Hindi (teacher) and he insisted that I first learn to write and I think he was right. I only knew how to write a little Gujarati and so I said to hell with starting again . . . and I was so busy. Now I ought to be starting again.[*]

● ● ●

ON MARRIAGE AND A PASSION FOR FLYING

JRD : Aviation and marriage came almost simultaneously because I started flying in 1929 and I got married in

---

[*] JRD was 79 years old when he said this.

December 1930. I decided in 1930, before we got engaged in May, to take on (the challenge of) the Aga Khan Trophy. So I went to England and back and I came back a hero, that sort of thing, which I think made her decide—whatever it was . . . so that was that.

The only important thing about my marriage was that it enabled me to see Kanchanjunga from close by. We went to Darjeeling in the winter, December, not realizing how cold it was, for our honeymoon. While there we didn't want to go to Tiger Hill. If you've been to Darjeeling you will know that all the tourists go to Tiger Hill at four in the morning to see the sunrise on a little white cone at a distance, which you're told is Mount Everest. Instead of that, we went off on a two-day jaunt, partly by horse, to Dhungroo and Sandakphu. Sandakphu is 12,000 feet up and there's nothing in front of you but a long valley and Kanchanjunga like a cathedral in front of you, and in fact what was most extraordinary was that the whole of the valley, the whole area, between Sandakphu where we were and right upto Kanchanjunga, was an uninterrupted layer of cloud—so the Kanchanjunga was sticking up by itself and what looked like a few miles away was really about forty miles away. It was so cold that we had to spend the night there with a wood-burning stove. Fortunately we found a lot of newspapers and so we wrapped our bodies with newspapers under our clothes to keep the cold out. And that was the occasion of the famous episode . . . .

He then spoke of how he and his wife intercepted the Bengal Governor's car in freezing weather near Darjeeling. On the way down the hill, the police stopped the car of JRD and Thelly. Even though it was a bitterly cold morning the police halted traffic for almost an hour. All this was to give the

Governor's car precedence. JRD and his wife decided to register their protest. They planned that when the Governor's car came into view, Thelly would step in front of it while JRD would give His Excellency a piece of his mind. It worked. Thelly and JRD boldly stepped in front of the Governor's car when it came up. When it stopped, JRD ran to the Governor's window and shouted: 'Who the hell do you think you are, keeping five hundred people, women and children, in the cold for an hour? You damn fool!' Thelly also wanted to give the Governor a piece of her mind, and rushed to the car window. Unfortunately, in the process, the Governor's car shot off. Among those shivering in the cold was a British Anglican priest. He came up to JRD and with all the dignity he could command, said, 'Sir, I do not approve of your language but I certainly approve of your sentiments.'

● ● ●

BEGINNING IN TATAS

JRD : I sat in Peterson's room in Navsari Chambers. Very ordinary room, ordinary cheap kind of table and chairs. You know, the kind of thing we have—solid but the real old type, no attempt to have decent padded furniture. I had a small desk at the end of his table. I must say that was a very formative and important time of my career. I saw a highly trained administrator, an ICS administrator like Peterson, and the way he was working. I learnt a lot from that.

I hadn't really the training to run a big group, which it was even then, though nothing like the size that it is now. For instance, when TELCO began I practically forced

Moolgaokar to come. I forced Sir Homi Mody who was hesitant to part with him at ACC. I said this is the man, we must get him. I realized, fortunately, that I didn't myself have the knowledge or the education, the formal education to run things myself—except, of course, Air India. I had no doubt about myself in Air India but I decided that where Tatas was concerned we must bring in people, top people, wherever we could, realizing that every company should have professional management. So in that sense I was the originator . . . not originator, but a believer long before, fifty years ago, of the need for independent, professional management for every company. Others didn't realize it but I did.

From 1970 onwards my status and my authority inevitably became diluted.*

* The Managing Agency system was abolished in April 1970 and thereafter technically each company was independent of Tata Sons.

THE BRITISH AND JRD

'During my early years in India,' said JRD, 'I had two personalities. I was an anti-British Indian and I was a Frenchman, a little more of a Frenchman than an Indian because French was my language.' (He surrendered his French citizenship in 1929.)

When he returned to India after his stint in the French army, his father took him to a Scotsman, the Director-in-Charge of Tata Steel. R.D. Tata said to John Peterson, 'John, I want you to train my son.' JRD said to me: 'What success I may have achieved in business I owe to one man, John Peterson, a burly Scotsman and a retired ICS official. It is from him that I acquired my love for English and my love for (English) poetry. He was remarkable in so far as he would be very polite to Indians and would go out of his way to help them. But he could be quite rough with his own people. When my father took me to him and asked him to train me as he was the Director-in-Charge of Tata Steel, Peterson put a desk for me in his room and for the next four or five years every paper that came to him came through me and every paper that went out went through me. He included me in every discussion and interview he had. It was from him that I acquired my qualities.'

Another Britisher he always spoke highly of was Nevill Vintcent, who helped him start his airline. After JRD died, I visited for the first time his rest room in the office. Apart from his father's portrait it had only one other photograph—

that of Nevill Vintcent.

We've read earlier about JRD's encounter with the British Governor in 1930. He once mentioned to me that perhaps it was because of that incident that he was put down in the British records as being anti-British. At one time he had three knights working under him. The British took their own time to probe him as to whether he would accept a knighthood. JRD showed no interest in the offer. His encounters with the Viceroy Lord Wavell are related in *Beyond the Last Blue Mountain.*

In the archival records one glimpses two instances where he stood up to the British in India. The first was when he spoke out for the air defence of India, an area he felt was sadly neglected by the British.

JRD played a leading role in whipping up support for Britain's war effort for the defence of India and spoke at meetings. At the time of the Battle of Britain, 1940, Tata Steel collected voluntary gifts and presented two Spitfires to Britain. In May 1941, JRD was proposing a word of thanks at a Rotary lunch after Group Captain W.W. Russell had spoken on the Air Defence of India, praising British efforts. JRD said: 'We are told that the Indian Air Force is being no less than quadrupled. Within a couple of years the skies of India will be clouded by the thundering mass of India's air squadrons. Four of them, fellow Rotarians! About thirty-six planes in all! Germany has lost more than three times as many in a few hours over England and both she and England are each building more than twice that number every day. We are told that we are training no less than three hundred pilots over a period of two years, that is, a hundred and fifty pilots a year. In Canada alone British and Dominion pilots are being trained at the rate of fifteen or twenty thousand a year. Need I say more.'

Writing in his half column, 'Dim' wrote in the *Bombay Chronicle* (28 May 1941): 'Top class, Mr Tata, top class. You will not be knighted if you go round town saying things like that, but you'll leave a name behind . . . .'

The second time JRD took a stand critical of the British was when he resigned from the Board of the Imperial Bank in Bombay. The cause for his displeasure was the discrimination against Indian officers that he perceived would continue even after World War II.

A copy of a letter, dated 2 April 1943, written by JRD to Sir William Lamond of the Imperial Bank was found in the archives of the Imperial Bank of India (now the State Bank of India). It shows that JRD was dissatisfied at the proportion of Indians in the bank's officer cadre (43 compared to 150 Europeans). Upon enquiring he found that Indians were completely excluded from high positions in the bank. He wrote: 'The insistence on reservation in the future of fifty percent of the senior posts for Europeans can only be justified by the assumption that Indians are inferior in ability to Europeans, or, if they have the ability, that they cannot be trusted. As an Indian I cannot accept either of these assumptions, and unless, therefore, I felt that they no longer governed the policy of the Board and of the Management, it would be unfair to myself and to the other Directors if I were to continue as a Member of the Board.'

● ● ●

ON THE BRITISH

RML : What was your relationship with the British in India?

JRD : So far as the highest level was concerned—the government, the high officials, the ICS, the typical John Peterson type—it was one of admiration for their intellect. At least for those people who came here as ICS officers and became government leaders and administrators in India, I admired, on the whole, their integrity, their honesty and so on. But, of course, I was always in angry opposition to their continuing as rulers. The top people were tops. The people in the middle jobs, the middle class, they were easily prone to racism, the feeling that 'how can Indians do anything as good as us, we are the superior people.' They felt that even with other Europeans. But that was not amongst the top people.

There's no doubt that the manner in which they responded to the war was superb. As people to deal with, I feel more attuned intellectually and emotionally to the British than to the Americans. I feel very much in tune with the French—but that's only intellectually.

● ● ●

LORD LINLITHGOW AND THE BULL

One of JRD's favourite stories involved Lord Linlithgow, Viceroy of India at the outbreak of World War II. The Viceroy was keen to upgrade the pedigree of Indian cattle and was going round a stud farm with Lady Linlithgow. The Viceroy was being shown around by the manager, followed by Lady Linlithgow with the assistant manager. The assistant manager pointed out the farm's stud bull to the Vicereine and said, 'Your Excellency, this is our champion bull. He performed three hundred and sixty-five times last year.'

'Is that so?' said Lady Linlithgow. 'You must go and tell His Excellency that.'

So the little man ran up to the Viceroy and, almost breathless, spluttered, 'Your Excellency, Your Excellency, Her Excellency wants me to tell you that this bull that we've just passed has performed *three hundred and sixty-five* times last year.'

'What! With the same cow?' roared Lord Linlithgow. 'No, Sir,' stammered the assistant manager. 'Go and tell that to Her Excellency,' replied the Viceroy firmly.

JRD had related to me another story about Lord Slim, details of which I had forgotten. The former British Prime Minister, Lord Callaghan, whom he had recounted it to, kindly sent me the story of General 'Bill' Slim at my request:

'Bill' Slim was a General and always insisted, as far as possible, on visiting the area nearest to the enemy. In the early part of the campaign against the Japanese in Burma, the Fourteenth Army was forced to retreat and General Slim decided to inspect the Allied forward positions. An Indian Major was delegated to accompany him.

They left at dusk to inspect three such posts. At each post the Indian Major whispered to General Slim the number of men holding the post, their armaments and so on. Finally General Slim enquired of the Indian Major in a whisper, 'How far are we from the Japanese lines?'

'About one thousand yards,' whispered the Indian Major. 'Then why on earth are we whispering!' 'Sir, I do not know why you are whispering,' replied the Major, 'but I have laryngitis.'

● ● ●

Conversations with JRD Tata

JRD once told me how he had 'saved the life' of the Duke of Edinburgh in Jamshedpur:

> When he came to Jamshedpur I received him at the airport with Sumant Moolgaokar and Joe Ghandy.* The whole town of Jamshedpur had been prepared to receive him. Thousands of children with little Union Jacks of paper. And we were to take him to TELCO, to the hospital, to the plant. To take him around, we needed an open car. And we found one. The Duke decided to sit on the back of the rear seat and put his feet on the seat so that he could be seen and could wave. Mr Moolgaokar decided that he would drive the car, though he had never driven that particular car. There were a lot of journalists, about twenty or thirty. They had apparently hired a truck and when he (Duke) saw them pulling up, he tapped Moolgaokar on the shoulder and said: 'Let's get the hell out of here.' He had a phobia of journalists. So Mr Moolgaonkar accelerated, let go the clutch, and the car jerked forward. Out of the corner of my eye I saw a pair of legs going up. The Duke was falling out of the car. We were accelerating and he would have fallen on his head. So I just grabbed the legs and brought him down. He thanked me.

---

* Sumant Moolgaokar was Director-in-Charge of Telco and Sir Jehangir (Joe) Ghandy, Director-in-Charge of Tata Steel.

TATAS

Personally humble, JRD was fiercely proud of Tatas. He often said, 'Tatas are different.' He told me that when any of his senior colleagues thought of taking a short cut even within the legal framework, he would tell them, 'Don't sail too close to the wind.' For him, what was good for India was good enough for Tatas.

I recall one of the Trust meetings where he said: 'Why do we spend most of our income on education and medical purposes? What does the nation need? What about urban slums and tribal development?' Words like 'What does the nation need?'came up so often with him. The word 'profit' hardly ever came up because that was not his primary motivation.

As the head of a large industrial house he needed to follow a policy of consensus. He usually included the chairmen of various Tata companies in the discussion of key issues even when they were not directly involved. It was a source of regret that some of his best chairmen were not so interested in Tatas as a whole as in their respective companies. Even so, he never gave up trying to get them thinking of the problems of the other companies in the conglomerate so that they would feel they were a part of Tatas as a whole and the group could benefit from their experience.

He seldom took solitary decisions and his policy of consensus made him include his colleagues frequently. When

I mentioned this to one of his long time colleagues, J.J. Bhabha, he proudly said of JRD, 'He is a democrat.' Another close colleague, S.A. Sabavala, added, 'Perhaps too much of a democrat,' and went on to relate how JRD would send drafts of important letters or documents to five or six of his colleagues and then attempt to incorporate their suggestions into his original. 'In the process,' Mr Sabavala said, 'the grandeur of his own concept was lost.' J. J. Bhabha noted that even after a decision was taken, if JRD was convinced it was incorrect and there was time to reverse it, he would never stand on his pride and would readily change it.

ARCHIVES

When a proposal for the Tata archives was put to him in 1990, JRD immediately responded positively. The question was finding space. I had heard that some space belonging to Tata Sons was available at Fort Chambers. So I asked JRD whether he could obtain it for the Archives. JRD rang up the Finance Director of Tata Sons, N.A. Soonawala, who kept an eye on the properties.

He preferred to talk from his speaker-phone without lifting the phone-receiver. He could amplify the volume and he found that more comfortable than a phone at his ear.

'Noshir, are you free to talk?'

'Yes, Sir.'

'I hear you are the proud owner of some office space which we need for our Archives.'

44

The Joy
of
Achievement

'Where is that?'

'Fort Chambers, ground floor.'

Soonawala laughed. He had kept that place under wraps for another project and said so.

When JRD put down the phone I remarked that he had quite a way of dealing with people, calling Soonawala 'the proud owner'.

'Why not?' asked Jeh.

I said, 'If anybody should be called an owner it is you as Chairman of Tata Sons.'

'Yes,' he said seriously, 'but he's *in charge!*'

Repeatedly I found how meticulous he was in respecting the authority of those who worked for him. He ordered his secretaries around but not his senior officials.

In some ways he was so busy making aviation history, he did not bother about the recording of it. It was only when the domestic airline and Air India were both nationalized and all the old records were handed over to the Government in 1953 that he realized what had happened. He said he did not have the foresight at that time to have an archive.

RML : It's understandable.

JRD : No, it's not. I should have. For instance, I didn't know when we created Tata Airlines that I was making history for India. To me it was just creating an airline, without any foresight that fifty years from now it would be important to know what we had done.

● ● ●

When J.N. Tata, the founder of Tatas, died, all he had to show the world were two highly successful textile mills and the enormous Taj Mahal Hotel. What he left behind, however, were his dreams for steel, hydro-electric power and the Indian Institute of Science, all of which were accomplished by his colleagues and successors. But perhaps more important were the standards and traditions Jamsetji left behind.

He said: 'We do not claim to be more unselfish, more generous or more philanthropic than other people. But we think we started on sound and straightforward business principles, considering the interests of the shareholders our own, and the health and welfare of the employees the sure foundation of our property.' Above all, it was Jamsetji's practice to think for the nation. JRD said that in several situations he would ask, 'How would J.N. Tata have looked at this issue? What would he have done?'

JRD spelt out Jamsetji's guidelines: 'What does this country need? It needs power, it needs steel, it needs scientific manpower. Even aviation, I (JRD) said. India cannot be without it. The whole world is going for it. I knew that flying was changing the world and India could not stay on the outside.'

JRD referred to Jamsetji Tata when we began discussing the biography I proposed to write. 'It seems obvious to me,' he said, 'that the fact that you would like to write a book on me means that you think I represent something more than I think I do. I am always comparing myself with others in India, or abroad or anywhere else, but I have no real concept. I don't believe what is said in the newspapers about me and I don't believe the sort of compliments I get; our country is very good at paying compliments; you get them all the time.'

RML : And not following the great man, whoever he is.

JRD : But I am not sure that I should be commanding your book. I hope that if you do write the book it will bring out a particular man, a character, a particular person. I don't know what's in your mind. You know, with Jamsetji Tata this would have been easier. He had two or three main features. A man of great intelligence; that is obvious, otherwise he would not have been Jamsetji Tata. A man of great vision. Now what is vision? Is vision a part of intelligence or a product of intelligence? Is vision something else, the interest or the ability to see things that are not there yet?

RML : An extension of intelligence. Some people's intelligence remains just intelligence.

JRD : Yes, but there are some very, very intelligent people who have no futuristic sense at all . . . .
Third, he definitely had a great sense of what needed to be done for the country . . . patriotism; not patriotism, rather he was patriotic, was willing to do something for his country. And finally, of course, great integrity. It can be integrity which is not only monetary integrity, because he was a rich man and why should a rich man be anything but honest, but a great integrity of thought and mind. And the final one is: a great humanity. The way he thought about workers— nobody did at that time. Or the care he took of people at Tata Steel, things like planting trees, flowering trees, and leaving room for schools and so forth. Quite remarkable and interesting.

R. D. Tata holding JRD
and Sooni Tata with Sylla

Sylla, Rodabeh and JRD

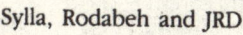

Sooni Tata with Jimmy in her arms and (from L to R) Rodabeh, JRD, Sylla and Darab

J. R. D. Tata with his wife Thelly and their two dogs Digby (left) and Pinnochio (right)

JRD in his sailor suit — his favourite photograph

JRD and Sylla in Japanese costume — Yokohama 1917,
where they spent a year and a half

JRD as a young man

The Taj Mahal Hotel where Sooni Tata stayed during her visit to India in 1916. Marked in the picture postcard for her mother is the suite they used on the right side and another room on the left

A picture postcard of Flora Fountain, Bombay, in 1904, the year JRD was born

Picture postcard of Marine Lines, Bombay, where Sooni Tata has
indicated the house where she and Ratanji stayed

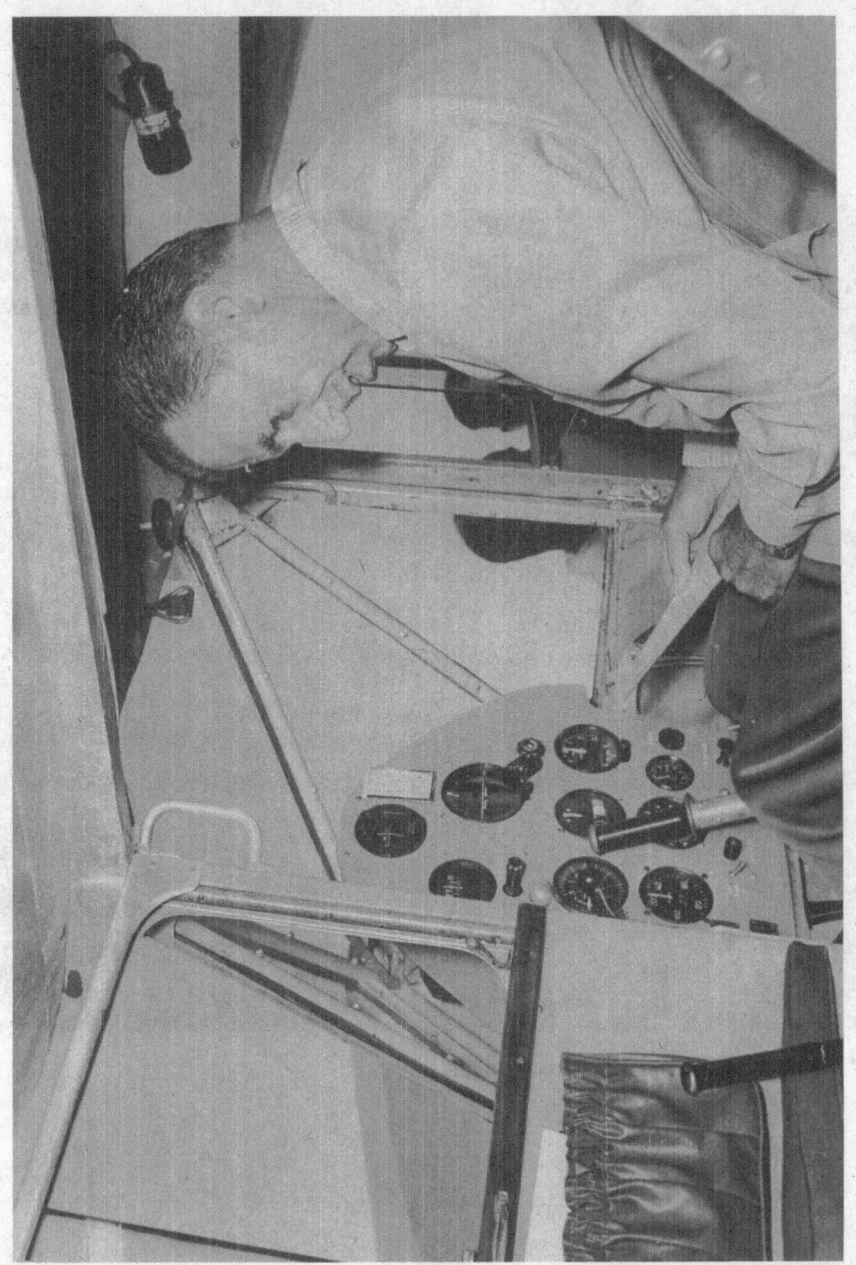

In the cockpit of a Leopard Moth in which he made his 30th Commemorative Flight Karachi/Bombay in 1962

On the occasion of the 50th anniversary flight

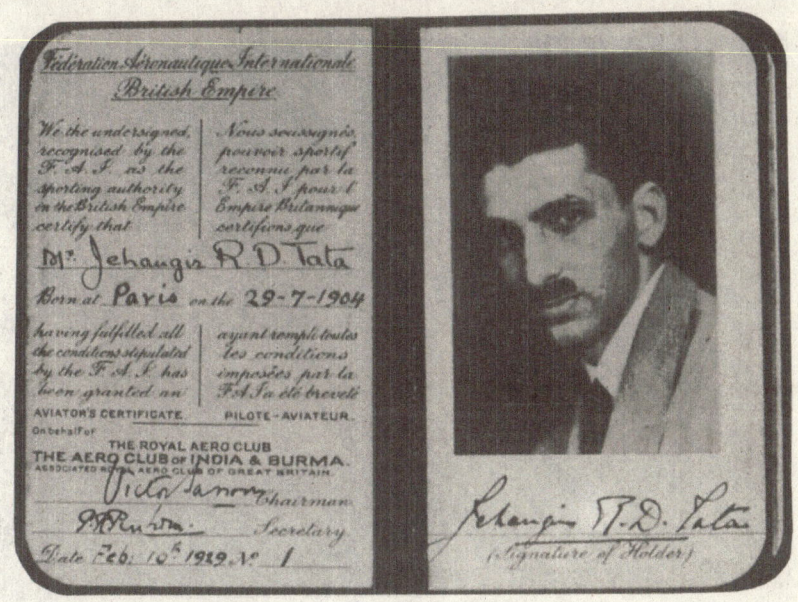

JRD.'s Pilot's licence No. 1.

Arrival of the inaugural mail flight from Karachi to Bombay,
October 15, 1932

JRD with Jawaharlal Nehru and his daughter, Indira, after a demonstration flight over the Himalayas in 1960

JRD with an Air India plane's cabin crew

At work in his office

JRD wanted companies to look beyond the welfare of their employees to those in their surrounding areas, encouraging them to learn crafts

JRD at Jamshedpur accompanied by H. P. Bodhanvala

JRD with the Duke of Edinburgh at the Oxford Study
Conference, 1956

JRD at the Tata Management
Training Centre, Pune, in the
early 60s

Dr. Homi Bhabha
introducing
JRD to Nobel Prize winner,
Dr. Neils Bohr, with
Jamshed Bhabha

In 1902, five years before even the site of the steel plant was located, Jamsetji Tata wrote to his son Dorab from abroad about what his dream city of steel should look like: 'Be sure to lay wide streets with shady trees, every other tree of a quick-growing variety. Be sure that there is plenty of space for lawns and gardens. Reserve large areas for football, hockey and parks. Earmark areas for Hindu temples, Mohammedan mosques and Christian churches.'

Over two decades later, in 1923, when Tata Steel experienced a crippling shortage of money, some shareholders accused the management of wasting money. JRD's father, R.D. Tata, replied: 'We are asked why it should be necessary to spend so much on housing, sanitation, roads, hospitals and welfare . . . . Gentlemen, we are not putting up a row of workmen's huts in Jamshedpur—we are building a city.'

● ● ●

RECALLING A SHAREHOLDERS' MEETING

In the 1920s and even in the 1930s, shareholders' meetings were small and were held in the offices of the respective companies after moving the furniture. JRD recalled an uproarious meeting of TOMCO (Tata Oil Mills) presided over by Sir Nowroji Saklatvala where about two hundred shareholders were present.

A disgruntled shareholder, Mr Shivdasani, addressed the meeting angrily and in his excitement pushed back the table in front of the directors. The directors—with all the dignity they could summon—drew their chairs back. An excited

Mr Shivdasani pushed the table further back. Finally he got so carried away that he climbed on to the table to harangue the shareholders.

'I enjoyed those meetings,' JRD chuckled.

● ● ●

LUNCHES AT BOMBAY HOUSE

JRD was reminiscing about lunch with the Directors in the 1940s and the 1950s in Bombay House, headquarters of Tatas.

JRD: Lunches with these two characters (Sir Homi Mody and Dr John Matthai) were hilarious. Sir Homi was bubbling with fun and Matthai, a Christian from Kerala, was constantly attacked (JRD meant teased) by him. Sir Homi referred to Matthai as 'Brother John' and at times as 'Brother-Praise the Lord-Matthai'.

On one occasion a well-known personality had died and Sir Homi said, 'Brother John, when we are dead, what will we be doing?'

Brother John pulled out his cigar and said: 'Roasting, I presume'.

JRD added, 'John Matthai was Chairman of Tata Chemicals and he got a bit fed up. And then I made him Vice-Chairman of Tata Steel. Then he was all right.' JRD said his real achievement was to get Matthai into the Bombay

'WHAT HAS BEEN THE DRIVING FORCE OF YOUR LIFE?'

RML : What has been the driving force of your life?

JRD : Honestly, if I had not been the son of R.D. Tata, one of the Tatas and the son of one of the main Tatas, if I had been, okay, maybe even a Godrej, I don't think I would have been so driven. I was driven by the fact that there was Jamsetji Tata in my life and that is what urged me to do things, to keep wanting to justify myself. I was very doubtful about my own capacity to follow these people. I had great admiration for my father, a little for Dorabji Tata,** an enormous amount for Jamsetji Tata and for what Tatas meant.

When I was a schoolboy, I was hoping one day that I would play polo and another day that, maybe, I would be a good tennis player, a racing-car driver; all the ordinary

---

* There is not much emphasis on the dangers of a rising population in the Bombay Plan (1943) though the Plan takes account of it. I once enquired whether it was the Bombay Plan that set him thinking about the danger of India's rising population, which he alerted India to in 1951 and consistently thereafter. JRD replied: 'I don't think so.' He could not say what exactly sparked his thinking on population.
** JRD admitted he got to know Sir Dorabji at the fag end of his life, when he was ill with diabetes. In his younger days, Sir Dorabji was a fine horseman and joined in the search for minerals in the distant jungles of India on a bullock-cart. In 1924, his readiness to sacrifice his personal fortune of Rs 1 crore, pledging it to the Imperial Bank, saved Tata Steel. He was not personally kind or caring towards JRD.

urges of young people, of children, of young boys who want to do something in their private lives. So, really, there was nothing that I did or showed signs of until I was suddenly put in a position where I was on test and was testing myself. From 1931 to 1938,* of course, I considered myself really on test. A little before, I started getting the idea that I might have to take more responsibility while Nowroji (Chairman) was still alive, but I never really thought of it. You know, we never think that people are going to die tomorrow. I said, well, maybe in five years. He was not very old.'

● ● ●

ON HIS TEMPER

Mr Shapoorji, who was later secretary to Sir Homi Mody, was occasionally called to take dictation by JRD in the late 1930s and early 1940s. He recalled, 'He (JRD) had a very hot temper then and would throw files at us. But kind-hearted. In those days we worked the whole of Saturdays and whenever there was a cricket match on a Saturday afternoon, JRD would call me and say, "Take half a day off."'

I asked JRD if this was true. He replied : 'I know I have a quick temper but I don't remember having ever flung files—even early in my career.'

In the later 1950s when Minoo Masani, once India's ambassador to Brazil, was first offered the post of JRD's executive assistant, he declined. Minoo was frank and said,

---

* From the last days of Sir Dorabji Tata till the death of Sir Nowroji Saklatvala and JRD's appointment as Chairman of Tata Sons

'Jeh, I value my relationship with you and I understand you bawl out people who are your executive assistants. I would rather not risk our friendship.'

JRD replied, 'But I know who to bawl out . I won't bawl you out.'

In keeping with his position of former ambassador, instead of calling him executive assistant, JRD gave Masani the French designation of 'chef de cabinet' (principal secretary). Rather hesitantly Minoo Masani agreed to accept the post. Two years later, when he stood for Parliament, Jeh insisted that Masani bid *au revoir* to Tatas and reluctantly Minoo did so. At their last meeting, JRD asked, 'Did I bawl you out?'

Although because of the pressure of work he could be quite short-tempered with the people closest to him, he more than made up for it with his care and affection for them. And in most cases his executive assistants became chairmen of various companies. And, whenever he went abroad, which was two to three times a year, he always remembered to get gifts for his two secretaries.

Despite his temper, he cared deeply for those who worked for him and was sensitive about the manner in which he corrected people, especially so in his later years. One Sunday morning when I went to his house, even before I could sit down he said: 'You will be unhappy but I must tell you that I saw your draft on . . . (some Trust matter) and I was not pleased with it.' He pointed out the specific paragraph.

I asked myself how many bosses would care to treat their deputies or staff members like that. His sensitivity to people sharpened as he mellowed with age. Soon after I joined Tatas, I had not attended to a certain matter promptly . He got a call from Paris that the PTA (Ticket) of a Professor he had invited had not reached Paris on time. He phoned me and inquired why there was a delay.

I said, 'May I come up and explain to you, Sir?'

'What explanation can there be?' he replied. 'The PTA had to go in time and the PTA has not gone in time.' Then, firmly, he added, 'This is *not* the way we work in Tatas.'

In later years he was more than generous with his compliments about my work but it was the chastizing that helped me the most.

● ● ●

APRES MOI

In 1988, we spoke extensively about the question people were asking : 'After J.R.D. Tata, what?' I enquired of JRD whether the question weighed on him.

'Not really. I have been asked that question often. If the organisation is sound it shall hold together.'

On one occasion he told me: 'They all gain in name by belonging to the Tata Group. There is no incentive, only disincentive in splitting up.' Then he enquired: 'Who will want to split it?'

Earlier, Ratan Tata had told me that JRD's personality had had a lot to do with holding Tatas together. 'He is very good at a one to one relationship.'

I asked JRD about his vision of Tatas in 2000 A.D. 'I would talk of the 21st Century and not of 2000 A.D. because that is only ten years away. But the work for that has to be done right now for it to fructify. I know what I want and Ratan will want that too—that we should be on the forward edge of the new developments and existing industries, which means that you will need to find outstanding scientists, managers, engineers. As I always say, "Give them a long rope".'

'What would you like Tatas to do?' I pressed.

'To be in the forward industries, where we have achieved, where we have the background, where we have the expertise. For example, we are in electric power, auto and associated industries like excavators. Tata Steel you will find is in the forefront of its field; it has excellent knowledge and expertise and greater cutting edge technologies not yet used.' He went on to mention the German Korf association with Tata Steel to make cement from slag thrown out by the steel companies, a technology that was being used only in Brazil in a small way. 'Tata Steel will be the first steel plant to use this process to produce the optimum quantity of cement.'

I mentioned that after him one could foresee four major empires—Tata Steel and its associate companies, the Chemicals group, the Indian Hotels, and Telco—in place of the present one with a number of other companies rotating around the parent company, Tata Sons, probably headed by Ratan Tata.

'There will also be the Electric Companies, and don't forget that the head of TISCO and TELCO will be the same,' he said, adding, 'Ratan Tata is the Deputy Chairman of TISCO and TELCO.' (Which he was at the time.)

JRD had carefully laid the groundwork for Ratan Tata to take over three years later in 1991.

● ● ●

SUCCESSION

JRD : I began to talk about it around 1960, 1970. Really 1970, after the abolishing of the Managing Agency when I was sixty (he was, in fact, sixty-five). It came to a definite decision in my mind at seventy that within the next few years, and I didn't think I'd wait till eighty, I must replace myself . . . .

Between 1987 and 1990 JRD used to occasionally talk about his desire to step down from Tata Sons. He talked of how he gave up the chairmanship of TELCO in 1972 and TISCO in 1984 but retained the chairmanship of Tata Sons 'because my colleagues tell me : "Stay on, stay on." And then I ask them, "Do you want me to go on until I go ga ga—and if I do, how would I know it?"' He paused and added, 'They replied to me, "Never mind, we will tell you".'

● ● ●

A WARRIOR'S HEART

Sometime in late 1991 or early 1992 when Tata Steel was going through a turbulent period, JRD said to me: 'If I live for two or three more years I'll see Ratan firmly in the saddle.'

At that time I was concerned whether his health could withstand the strain of the events. I was surprised to see how well he took it. Behind the bodily weakness of a man in his late 1980s, there was still the heart of a warrior.

By April 1993 the air had cleared. As he was going to lunch one day I accompanied him down the corridor and quoted William Cowper's lines:

His purposes will ripen fast
Enfolding every hour;
The bud may have a bitter taste,
But sweet will be the flower.

He stopped abruptly. 'Say that again', he ordered firmly. I did. Thoughtfully and silently he walked to his lunchroom.

● ● ●

CHANGE OF GUARD

In the senior officer's lunchroom of Bombay House, every Monday the Taj serves us Western style chicken as the main dish. On Monday, 25 March 1991, we found rice, dal, fish *patia* and yoghurt and *sev* (fried vermicelli) for dessert—a menu reserved for festive Parsi occasions. We asked our waiter Lucas whose birthday we were celebrating. Lean, tall and blunt, he looked down at us at the table condescendingly and said the festive fare was being served 'because today Mr J.R.D. Tata is handing over charge to Mr Ratan Tata.' We stared at each other—humbled at the confirmation of our belief that at Bombay House the best informed are the waiters, the peons, the drivers.

When I returned to my office and announced the news, a lady said proudly: 'But he will always be our Chairman.'

Ten days later, when I met JRD on 5 April, he spoke of Ratan spontaneously : 'He pleases and surprises me with his memory for events. He has a very good memory and in my job you have got to have a good memory.'

As he was in a mood to speak of Ratan I asked him what other qualities of his successor appealed to him—integrity, perhaps?

'Yes, definitely. But I don't want to use that word because

it could be taken to mean that others don't have it. Integrity, with leadership . . . (I would say). He has an understanding of modern science and technology. None of my other colleagues have it except Darbari Seth. Ratan has a modern mind. He has great energy—for example for tedious flying. He said he would come with me to America to the hospital (where JRD was going for his angioplasty operation). I said he should not. I am very easy in hospital. I don't want anybody in the hospital except nurses and a good doctor.' Ratan Tata did go to be with him.

JRD continued: 'Ratan has everything I want for the firm. He has integrity, memory, energy—integrity of my type. Ratan realizes that in a letter he has written to me. He says, "You set yourself higher standards of integrity than anyone else I know in the manner in which you have conducted yourself."' Then he showed me Ratan Tata's two-page handwritten letter to JRD on his retirement as Chairman of Tata Sons a few days earlier.

● ● ●

WHEN RATAN TATA BECAME CHAIRMAN

After he took over as Chairman of Tata Sons, Ratan Tata related to me that although there was talk for a long time of his being appointed Chairman of Tata Sons, when it finally happened, it came as a surprise to him.

This is how it happened. JRD had just been discharged from hospital and was in his office where Ratan saw him on 18 March 1991. As soon as he entered, JRD asked,

'What's new?' Ratan Tata said he was a bit taken aback and replied: 'Jeh, I have already been informing you in hospital of all that is happening. What else can be new?' JRD replied: 'In that case I have something to tell you.' Then JRD mentioned that his thought was to step down and he wanted to propose Ratan's name as the Chairman. He added, 'But first I'll have to consult Ajit Kerkar.'

'Why Kerkar?' asked a surprised and somewhat annoyed Ratan. 'Because he will let me know the auspicious date!' replied JRD. That is why the Tata Sons Board meeting due on Wednesday, 27 March, was shifted to Monday, 25 March.

AIR INDIA

BOAC AND AIR INDIA

Jeh said his relationship was somewhat coloured by the days of the Independence struggle (especially after he attended the Quit India Resolution Meeting of the Congress). About six years later came the question of starting Air India operations in England.

JRD : A top British Aviation official came to India, when we had started operation in England but had not yet gone to America. He (the British official) said in a very charming way, 'You know, Mr Tata, we don't think that Heathrow is really suitable for Air India.' Instead, he offered the big international airport between Glasgow and Edinburgh. So I just replied, 'It is kind of you to say so but we feel the same about BOAC and Bombay and Delhi. During the war, large airfields were prepared in India and there is a big one in Central India—Nagpur or Hyderabad—and we feel that is where we should show you the same consideration.' He just looked at me and laughed. But he was quite serious when he was talking. He thought he could bully us since we were new in the airlines business.

RML : Who helped you?

JRD : We were absolutely on our own. Every country we went to we had to give reciprocity. So I never had any special close friendship with anybody important in England except Callaghan (ex-Prime Minister of Britain). I liked Callaghan. Somehow we met three times and at one dinner at the Government House I told a couple of stories and Callaghan was absolutely charmed with them and he wrote me a letter thanking me for giving him useful stories that he had made proficient use of.

● ● ●

HOW THE AIRLINE BEGAN

JRD : Somebody told him (Nevill Vintcent who was giving joy rides in India), 'Why don't you see JRD Tata? He's just taken up flying.' Nevill Vintcent came to me and I enthusiastically took to him. He was remarkable. A very fine man.

RML : What was your first impression when he walked into your office? It was a historic meeting.

JRD : Don't forget, he had been a heavy-weight champion of boxing, heavy-weight champion of the Middle East, Royal Air Force (during World War I). He was a powerful man. Once, at night, they had to force land in the desert and had to spend the night there. They (he and his navigator) were surrounded by a hostile Arab tribe. In order to give his navigator a field to fire with the machine gun which was firing forward only (as it was fixed), Vintcent got out, picked up the rear of the plane and put it on his shoulder and then moved to the right and left and (the navigator) kept on aiming and firing. This needed a lot of physical strength, which he had the physique for . . . .

RML : A car is one thing but a plane!!!

JRD : And the courage too! In India, his colleague and he had been going up and down the country giving joy rides. They had flown all the way from England in that plane. He was studying everything possible and considering the scope for starting an airline. He knew, the man that he was, that the Imperial Airways Airline was coming to India, to Karachi, as a first step towards Australia. That was the ultimate aim, but they would also go across to Delhi and Calcutta. The whole of south India would be blank and unserviced and that's how he worked out a proposal to have a flight from Karachi to Ahmedabad to Bombay and to Madras. With those planes, we had to stop for the night.

We started a service to Delhi. We were going to expand, and J.D. Choksi (legal advisor of Tatas) advised that now there should be a new arrangement with Mr Vintcent. I was inclined to accept Mr Choksi's advice. Vintcent said 'No'. He was of the view that an agreement could not be broken. Mr Choksi felt that the agreement was not a perpetual one and that it should be re-negotiated. And Vintcent said 'No' and that he was going to go. I was very uncomfortable and I felt, 'No, Nevill is right and Choksi is wrong.' And in any case, it was not a legal matter, it was a question of what is fair. It was true that we (Tata Airlines) had become very large with figures running into lakhs of rupees a year, whereas when we started it was a few thousand. So I went to a lawyer I trusted, called Dinshaw Daji, an old man, who was a director of one of our companies. I always found him a man whom everyone respected. A little peculiar, he always used to wear his *feta* (Parsi cap) at an angle, moving it forward and backward from time to time. The other peculiarity about him was that he never sat down to work. He worked at an easel, standing up. He said he couldn't work sitting down. So I put the case to Dinshaw Daji and I told him, 'Look, this is the problem and I'm uncomfortable and I don't know, my colleagues think that this is right. I want your advice.' He said that Nevill was right. So I immediately came back and took it upon myself and told Nevill, 'Nevill, forget it, you're not going.' And that was it.

RML : But your colleagues, you must have had quite a job persuading your colleagues. (JRD was not the Chairman then.)

JRD : No—I didn't have to because I was very firm about it. I feel guilty (that he didn't stand up earlier for Nevill Vintcent).

RML : So you took a moral stand on the issue.

JRD : I said we shouldn't go into the legal aspects of a situation like this. It was the moral aspect—that Tatas have always respected. And nobody said 'No'.

JRD : My devotion to Aviation was not only to the airline but to aviation and aeroplanes.

JRD then went on to say how he had always wanted to make an aeroplane and related his two abortive attempts to do so during World War II. The first was to manufacture a Mosquito twin-engined fighter bomber and the second was to build gliders for the war front. The first was aborted because, said JRD, someone in the British Government was shrewd enough to realize that once the Indians got the knowhow, they would be able to compete with British aviation interests. On the gliders, JRD questioned the British Government how they planned to transport them all the way from Poona to the Burma border. That ended the glider experiment!

● ● ●

TATA AIRLINES

When it started in October 1932 it had only three pilots : JRD, Nevill Vintcent and one other.

In its report on the first year of Tata Airlines' operations, the Directorate of Civil Aviation, New Delhi, noted :

As an example of how airmail service should be run, we commend the efficiency of Tata Services who on October 10, 1933, arriving at Karachi as usual to time, completed a year's working with 100 per cent punctuality . . . . Even during the most difficult monsoon months when rainstorms increased the perils of the Western Ghat portion of the route no mail from Madras or Bombay missed connection at Karachi nor was the mail delivered late on a single occasion at Madras . . . . Our esteemed Trans-Continental Airways, alias Imperial Airways, might send their staff on deputation to Tatas to see how it is done.

Speaking about those years JRD said:

I was tense only when there was bad weather. Tenseness in my case of pushing through, perhaps because I was so anxious that the mail should not be delayed. So maybe on some occasions I would push through when I could have turned back.

Flying through bad weather in the planes in those days with very few instruments was quite a job. Sometimes I think to myself, 'Funny, I must have been a natural pilot.' I have read magazines in which it is reported that a number of accidents take place when people get disorientated in clouds, which can happen very easily if you do not have the instruments. And I used to fly through clouds deliberately sometimes but never remember an occasion when I felt I was disorientated. But it is true I have done unsafe operations. I have flown during the monsoon, I have landed in fields. But once you begin to operate an airline you have to be responsible.

● ● ●

AVIATION SIDELIGHTS

JRD was proud of his licence No. 1. He made it a point, however, to say that he was not the first candidate to enrol at the Bombay Flying Club, only the first to pass out. He told Mr Frederick Philips (then Chairman of the multinational Philips) that although some people called him the 'Father of Civil Aviation', it was more appropriate to call him the 'Grandfather', given his age! Philips, a couple of years older than him, was also a keen flyer and a few years earlier had flown in his private plane to India, taking over the controls when landing and taking off.

64

When Mr Philips related that even after he stepped down as President of his organisation his successors were kind enough to permit him the use of his room, JRD said, 'I hope they will do the same with me.' He had hopes but no demands of his successor. [*]

It was typical of JRD that whenever he talked on aviation and someone was loading him with compliments, he would give credit to 'a very fine Englishman', Nevill Vintcent, who had first proposed the airline to him, worked with him for ten years as a partner and died in an aircrash in the Bay of Biscay during the World War. Though friends like J.D. Choksi of Tatas were very close to him in Tatas and he had much affection for them, in later years whenever he made references to his old colleagues, it was his friends in the airlines about whom he spoke with the most affection. JRD had flown several generations of planes from the wood and fabric single engine Puss Moth and Leopard Moth to the steel-bodied Boeing. In 1949, JRD flew the Vampire jet, then the fastest plane in the world at 540 m.p.h. Bobby Viccaji relates how one day an aircraft suddenly swept very low over an airfield they were visiting in England. A director belonging to the aircraft manufacturers, Havilland, exclaimed, 'Good God! Geoffrey Havilland must be in that plane.'

It was not. It was JRD having the time of his life.

● ● ●

* Not only did he continue to use his room till the end of his life but his successor Mr R. N. Tata has asked that the room with its original contents be replicated in the Tata Central Archives, Pune, so people can have a glimpse of it.

From 1938 to 1978, for forty years, JRD was head of the largest industrial house in the country while simultaneously running Tata Airlines, which became Air India in 1946. In 1948 he launched Air India International. How did he manage his work schedule? How did he divide his time? JRD had the great gift of shifting dexterously from one subject to a totally unrelated one and giving equal attention to both. He could compartmentalize his mind and bring to bear all his concentration on the subject or the company he was dealing with. At the height of his responsibilities he had six in-trays of papers. These were of Tata Sons and Tata Industries; TISCO; TELCO; Air India; Miscellaneous; Newspapers and Magazine cuttings.

Only very urgent papers would be kept on his desk. His desk was arranged with meticulous care and necessary items like stapler and scissor were near at hand; destapler, pencils, pen, pad, which were in frequent use, were within easy reach and in the order in which he needed them. Only in the last two or three years of his life did his power to switch from one subject to another slow down and he would often ask, 'Say it again.'

RML : Did you attend to Air India work in the Air India office or in Tatas?

JRD : Air India about once or twice a week, if there was any reason to.

RML : How did you divide your time between these two?

JRD : By God, sometimes upto half my time was devoted to Air India.

RML : Did you work on Air India in the mornings and pick up Tata work in the afternoons?

JRD : No. I used to have meetings with the Manager of Air India or the Chief Accountant or Bobby Kooka (in Bombay House). If there was anything to do with the decor of the planes, or meetings with the pilots, meetings with the engineers, the unions—then those would always be held in Air India.

JRD's driver Peter told me that if JRD went to Air India Building at Nariman Point in the morning and said he would come down by lunchtime and then changed his plans to lunch at Air India, he would come down the twenty-four floors to tell him. He would never send just a message for the driver.

● ● ●

DIFFERENCE BETWEEN MANAGING AIR INDIA AND TATA STEEL

JRD : Don't forget, Air India was particularly important to me. It was an operation in which I did have the feeling that my judgement would prevail. I always took the views of others but the final decision was mine. With Tatas the organization was already in place and I think there was a need for a consensus. When you are dealing with very, very large organisations you have got to be careful that you don't take a line where you destroy or damage something that has taken years to build. With Air India I was creating something new, something entirely new, and therefore I was creating history in a small way and so did not have to have the responsibility for the past. I could afford to make mistakes without undoing the good that was done by others in the past that would create hardship for a large number of people.

In Tata Steel, when I came into Tata Steel it was a creation of Jamsetji Tata. I couldn't throw my weight around there—there were so many important people, intellectually powerful people whose judgement I respected.

● ● ●

BOBBY KOOKA

RML : Bobby Kooka.* You allowed him to crack jokes at your expense and your (Tata) directors' expense in a Tata house magazine. Nobody in the world would have allowed it. Why did you allow it? He made fun of you and the top directors like J.D. Choksi.

JRD : Particularly J.D. Choksi and also the father of General Bewoor (former Chief of Staff of the Indian Army), Sir Gurunath Bewoor, who was a high ICS officer of the Government before joining us. He was in charge of Air India and Bobby took rather a liking to him and he used to call him 'Guru-Buru'—I don't know why. There were always some cartoons about 'Guru-Buru'. But there were some fellows who took a dislike to Bobby, like Kaikaus Madan, the Financial Manager of Tata Steel. He (Bobby Kooka) always made fun of him. But he made friendly fun of Choksi.

---

*   Head of Traffic and Publicity for Air India, he was one of JRD's closest colleagues in the Airlines for almost forty years.

He didn't think that Choksi was as outstanding as I thought him to be. He even made fun of me. But you couldn't request Bobby to go easy on people—you either stopped him completely or you let him be.

● ● ●

HURT

The part of his working life when he was at his creative best was also a time of frustration as he steered the ship of Tatas through the shoals of permits and licences. But yonder in the sky the sun of Air India warmed him. His bound spirit could escape and reach the stars. Till one day a Prime Minister—Morarji Desai—in a capricious act plucked him out of the sky. The wound was all the greater for the way it was done. He wasn't even warned.

He was human enough to be hurt. He never quite recovered from the way he was 'fired', as he called it, from Air India. When he saw Prime Minister Morarji Desai on 24 January 1978, Morarji never raised with him the point of retirement, but on 3 February, when the Air India Board was reconstituted, his name did not feature. Without telling JRD, who had founded and headed Air India for thirty years, Morarji Desai asked Air Chief Marshal P.C. Lal (Retd.), whom JRD had appointed Managing Director of a medium-sized Tata company in Jamshedpur, to take over. P.C. Lal rang up JRD from Delhi to break the news.

'And, what did you reply?' JRD demanded of P.C. Lal.

'What could I say to the Prime Minister?' P.C. Lal replied

feebly.

In the nine o'clock news on 3 February 1978, it was announced that Air Chief Marshal P.C. Lal had taken over the Chairmanship of Air India from Mr J.R.D. Tata. It hurt JRD no end.

What was worse was to have Morarji Desai write to say, 'We are sorry to part with you,' after the way he was 'fired'. After twenty-five years of service to the government he expected the courtesy to be informed directly and not through his successor and the nine o'clock news-bulletin.

Three years after this incident, in 1981, when I showed JRD a copy of my book, *Encounters with the Eminent*, which featured him among others, he went down the list of personalities. As soon as he saw Morarji Desai's name he asked with contempt, 'Why Morarji?'

He shut the book and put it down somewhat forcefully on the table.

● ● ●

AIR INDIA

RML : Fali Nariman (the well-known advocate of the Supreme Court) who has great regard for you told me, 'Even Jeh is human and he was so keen to get back on the Board of Air India after he was thrown out.' Is that true?

JRD : Yes, only in the sense that all the staff and the top people came to me and said, 'Sir, nothing is being done except through the ministry—for God's sake come back'. But I never said or asked anything from 1978 to 1982—

until I did a slightly tricky thing, the 1982 flight,* four years after I'd been fired. I was interviewed by the press and they talked about Air India. I said, 'Why do you talk to me about Air India? I'm not on the Board of Air India.' They didn't know that I was no longer on the Board. So immediately one or two articles appeared, saying it is strange that Mr Tata who had just done this dangerous thing etc. etc. Almost the next week, Mrs Gandhi put me on the Board! But otherwise, no, I was keen (on rejoining) in the sense only of trying to meet an intense request of the staff.

---

* On October 15, 1982, on the 50th Anniversary of Air India, JRD undertook a Commemorative Flight in a vintage Leopard Moth of the early 1930s along the old mail route from Karachi to Bombay via Ahmedabad.

THE ART OF MANAGEMENT

The art of management makes all the difference between heaven and hell. In heaven, the policemen are English, the cooks are French, the artists are Italian, and the administrators are Swiss. In hell, the policemen are French, the cooks are English, the artists are Swiss, and the administrators are Italian.

—A quotation found in the papers of JRD

When asked about his approach to people management, JRD said that he had made mistakes like everybody else. For instance, he said, he had been criticized for being too much of a consensus man. He admitted that he did not like taking unilateral decisions.

JRD : I am disinclined to take hard decisions because they would create unpleasantness. But I personally feel, though I may be wrong, that keeping a certain constancy in the way people regard you, in the way you relate to people will result in a good net result over the long term. You know, it is like a family. You can't take strong, hard decisions throughout, fire so and so, get rid of so and so, back up one side of the family rather than another. I know that all my

colleagues have their own views and on many views of
theirs I don't agree and they don't agree perhaps with mine.
But, generally, we have always come to feel that we are
doing the best that we can and that we are sincere and
that we mean to do the right thing.

• • •

GETTING THE BEST OUT OF OTHERS

JRD : When a number of persons are involved I am definitely
a consensus man. But that does not mean that I do not express
my views. But basicallly it is a question of having to deal with
individual men heading different enterprises. And with each
man I have my own way. I am one who will make full
allowance for a man's character and idiosyncrasies. You
have to adapt yourself to their ways and deal accordingly
and draw out the best in each man . . . . It may be that
because all others were older than me when I became the
chairman (at thirty-four) I became a consensus man. . . . If
I have any merit, it is getting on with individuals according
to their ways and characteristics. At times it involves
suppressing yourself. It is painful but necessary . . . . To be
a leader you have got to lead human beings with affection.

• • •

JRD'S GOLDEN RULE FOR SUCCESS

JRD had one rule that he said was essential for anything

worthwhile to be achieved—'Strive for perfection and you will reach excellence.' I once asked him what the secret of his success in business was. He shook his head. 'No secret, just long hours. I used to put in seventy-five to eighty hours of work a week.' He then added rather mischievously, 'You know something? I do not like work. I like to be interrupted.'

● ● ●

GUIDING PRINCIPLES

When a teacher in Calcutta asked JRD to list his 'guiding principles', he summarized them as follows:

Nothing worthwhile is ever achieved without deep thought and hard work.

One must think for oneself and never accept at face value slogans and catch phrases to which, unfortunately, our people are too easily susceptible.

One must forever strive for excellence, or even perfection, in any task, however small, and never be satisfied with second best.

No success or achievement in material terms is worthwhile unless it serves the needs or interests of the country and its people and is achieved by fair and honest means.

Good human relations not only bring great personal rewards but are essential to the success of any enterprise.

● ● ●

HOW JRD SAW HIMSELF

JRD : I had no training in management but when I started in 1926, some books on management were being written. Not having had an academic training in engineering and technology, my only contribution to management had to be in handling men who had been so trained. Every man has his own way of doing things. To get the best out of them is to let them exploit their own instincts and only intervene when you think they are going wrong. Therefore all my management contributions were on the human aspect through inducing, convincing and encouraging the human being. The exception was in the field of aviation, where I knew the technical side and perhaps half my love for aviation comes from the fact that it was the only field in which I have felt competent.

One thing I regret is never having been in line-management except in the airlines. In other fields decisions I took had to be executed by someone else. As I had no technical training, I always liked to consult the experts. At times I felt like a soldier who has never been an officer catapulted to be a General. When I have to make a decision I feel I must first make sure that the superior knowledge of my advisers confirms the soundness of my decision; secondly, that they would execute my decision not reluctantly but being convinced about it; thirdly, I see myself in Tatas as the leader of a team, who has to weigh the impact of any decision on other Tata companies, on the unity of the group. I think this policy has paid off.

• • •

A STICKLER FOR PROPRIETY

In the 1940s, the late Vasant Sheth, (who rose to become Chairman of Great Eastern Shipping Co.) was in college. He was waiting at a bus stop with three other friends, two of them girls. An owner-driven cream Chrysler New Yorker drove up and the driver inquired if anyone would like a lift. Vasant Sheth was the only one to recognize who the occupant of the car was. He hustled his companions into the back and settled himself next to the driver. To impress his lady friends, Sheth turned to them and said with some deliberation, 'Do you know whose car we're travelling in?' And answered himself: 'We are travelling in the car of Mr J.R.D. Tata.'

The driver turned to Sheth and said, 'Young man, this car does not belong to J.R.D. Tata. It belongs to the Tata Iron and Steel Company.'

This distinction between what was his and what belonged to the company was something Vasant Sheth never forgot when he reached a high position himself.

• • •

PLANNING FOR A NATION

At the height of World War II, JRD, then only thirty-nine,

got together some of the top industrialists of India to think how the economic structure of the country could be recreated after the War. The industrialists he invited were G.D. Birla, Kasturbhai Lalbhai, the textile mill-owner from Ahmedabad, Sir Purshottamdas Thakurdas from Bombay and Sir Shri Ram from Delhi. The technocrats were all from Tatas—Sir Ardeshir Dalal, A.D. Shroff and Dr John Matthai. The plan came to be known as the Bombay Plan or the Tata-Birla Plan. When the Bombay Plan was published (in two instalments) in 1943 and 1944, it created a stir.

The distinctive feature of the Bombay Plan was that for the first time in the world a group of industrialists were planning for a nation. Speaking about it JRD said: 'I can't take credit for more than being the first businessman to see the need for the Plan. It went on to planning but it started with a feeling that Indian businessmen must prepare themselves for what was to happen after the War . . . when India became free, as I was sure it would, and we must do something to develop the country. It was (to start with) only a committee of businessmen . . . (I thought) there must be a role for us—we must accelerate development. Then in the course of deliberations came the idea of planning in the modern sense . . . . I knew independence was bound to come; I knew the country's economy would have to be tackled—that economic prosperity needed to reach not only the few but the many. Businessmen and not only the government should play a role.'

He went on to mention an event that was to prove a watershed in his life. 'Till I went to the Congress meeting, I thought this freedom movement could not work but then I saw the real impact of Gandhi backed by Nehru. I didn't know (Sardar Vallabhbhai) Patel then. I knew that the English would be economically destroyed by the War. I always took an interest in history—contemporary history, ancient Greece and more of Rome—that excited me. Later on, the Napoleonic era. Taking the historical view I knew England could never hold on to the empire after the War.'

He went on to speak of G.D. Birla's contribution to the Plan: 'G.D. Birla was a man of high intelligence and knowledge. When we were floundering to find a structure in the first few meetings, it was he who suggested: "It is difficult to forecast what India should do after being free . . . .So let's do it this way—first estimate to get the people the kind of standard of living that they want. What is needed? So many calories of food requiring so many millions of tons of grain, so many metres of cloth, housing— how many cubic feet of housing, so many schools, etc." The concept of quantifying made it easy and it was on that basis that Dr Matthai wrote the Plan.'

LITERATURE & SPORT

In *Keynote* JRD spoke of his lifelong love affair with the English and French languages as also of his desire 'to live a little dangerously'. This section covers these two interests of his life.

All his life JRD kept a thin red scrapbook where he jotted down select poems in French and English from 1924 onwards along with occasional sayings that interested him, both witty and profound.

● ● ●

LOVE FOR POETRY

JRD : I was always interested, of course, in languages, in anything that was well-worded in English or in French. So I began to read poetry. When I joined the army, I discovered it was a very dull life; an ordinary soldier in the French Army, you can imagine. I decided to read, so I got hold of a book of poetry and I bought an exercise book and I decided to write down the poems that I liked. I started with a few, then kept it up for about five years. Later on, I occasionally added to it, but I didn't have the time to illustrate it. Then when I came to India I started this scrapbook in 1925. When I came here I started reading English poetry and would put down the things that I liked, but I have added very few. When I read a poem that pleased me or enthralled me, I wanted to be able to repeat it or see it again, so I put it down. I should have continued. If ever I get time I shall do it again. I have kept spaces for illustrating some of them. The drawings are, of course, totally unrelated to the subject. It is only to beautify the book or to amuse me.

● ● ●

JRD READS FROM O'HENRY

One Sunday morning when I saw him, there was a headline in the papers that a wealthy jeweller's son had been kidnapped for ransom. The subject of ransom cropped up casually in the conversation and his face lit up. He enquired if I had read O' Henry's 'The Ransom of Red Chief'. He then went on to relate the story which was set in a small town in America in the the late nineteenth century. Two kidnappers desperate for money decide to kidnap the only son of the wealthiest man in the town. The kidnapping goes according to plan and they take the ten-year-old boy out of town and send the father a claim for a ransom of $1500. Far from being upset, the little boy seems to enjoy his outing. One of the two kidnappers becomes his horse and he is the big Red Chief riding on him, while the other kidnapper tries to negotiate terms with the father. The little boy goes from one game to another till the 'horse' kidnapper becomes a nervous wreck. What the kidnappers hadn't known, but are discovering, is that the brat was the terror of his neighbourhood.

At this point JRD picked up a well-thumbed copy of O' Henry's complete stories and read out the reply of the wealthy father of the boy:

> Gentlemen, I received your letter today by post, in regard to the ransom you asked for the return of my son. I think you are a little high in your demands, and I hereby make you a counter-proposition, which I am inclined to believe you will accept. You bring Johnny home and pay me two hundred and fifty dollars in cash, I agree to take him off your hands. You had better come at night, for the neighbours believe he is lost, and I couldn't be responsible for what they would do to anybody they saw bringing him back. Very respectfully.

Late at night, the poor kidnappers take the boy back to his father, much against the little fellow's wishes, and dig into their meagre resources to pay the $250. Then, terrified that the neighbours will lynch them for bringing the pest back, the kidnappers run for their lives right across the US into Canada!

JRD went on to relate another O' Henry story; it seemed almost as if he was a witness to the episode : 'A disappointed girl. She really doesn't want to live. She's ill. She lives in a very poor room in New York. Outside the window all she can see is a wall and on the wall there is a creeper. The leaves are falling—it's autumn. There is an old janitor who tries to make her eat something and helps her—he's very fond of her and feels very sorry for her. She tells him that when the last leaf on the creeper falls she'll die. That night, when she's not looking, the old man climbs a ladder and paints a leaf on the wall, so one leaf will never fall. She survives because she's always looking for the leaf and the leaf is always there. So she survives. But he dies of pneumonia.'

When asked, 'Is he (O' Henry) your favourite author?' JRD replied: 'He and the Frenchman (Saint Exupéry, who wrote *Night Flight from Arras* and *The Little Prince*).' On one of the early occasions I met him he loaned me his copy of *The Little Prince* and suggested I read it. At one time he also said he liked 'the author who shot himself (Hemingway)' and had read most of the books by Louis Lamour.

'All short stories,' he said as he picked up his volume of O'Henry. 'Small type. This contains the complete works. You cannot get this. I don't know if they're available anywhere.' I later bought him a modern omnibus O' Henry with better types but he said it was not as complete and continued for several years with his old favourite copy.

RML : What are your favourite O' Henry stories?

JRD : 'Road to Destiny', 'Ferby', 'Double-Die Deceiver', 'Whistling', 'Dicks Christmas Stockings', 'The Ransom of Red Chief'.

He said sometimes he read an O'Henry story to his wife.

One evening, a few months before he died, he said his sister Sylla's grandson Jehangir and his wife Laila were coming and they would read O'Henry stories together. 'He is good at reading, so am I and so is his wife.'

● ● ●

❦

The Joy
of
Achievement

When JRD started in Tata Steel in 1926 he was only twenty-two. French, not English, was his mother tongue. As a result, he found dictating in English difficult. By dint of effort, he mastered English and soon came to love the language. For years, he was an avid reader of 'Increase your Word Power' in *Reader's Digest*. While editing *Keynote*, I sat with him as he corrected his Foreword. He chose his words with great care and proved to be an excellent editor as well. 'Just as well, Sir, you are not in the editing field,' I observed. 'You would put us all out of business.' He smiled.

He wrote in *Keynote*: 'I don't mind admitting also to a number of continuing love affairs: a lifelong one with the languages, literature and poetry of France and England, which makes me wish that more of the little formal education I have had had been in one of the rich and beautiful languages of our own country.' He stated, '(the) excuse for my correcting mania lies in my abiding love for the English language, so often profaned in our country.' He would never stop trying to improve what he had written, and this habit once led Dr John Matthai to observe: 'When are you going to stop ill-treating your drafts.'

JRD said to me on one occasion: 'My first stenographer, Iyer, was the stenographer of Mr Peterson and he was the chief stenographer of Tata Steel. Very nice, very quiet old man. As I did very little dictating in those days, I used to write out my draft. Noticing this, Peterson said, "Look, you must get into the habit of dictating, otherwise one takes more time." But some people can't dictate at all and I certainly couldn't. I was terrified of dictating, so when I'd send for Iyer to dictate a letter, I'd first write the letter, conceal it underneath my desk (unknown to Iyer) and read

from it to give myself confidence.* After a time I became so
proficient at dictation that now I just cannot write. Actually,
I do continue to write letters, but I much prefer to dictate
because then I can change; you can't change a letter when
you write by hand, you can only make a draft. If you write
a letter to somebody it's a nuisance to have to rewrite it,
particularly if it's four pages long.

● ● ●

GOLF

RML : When did you stop playing golf?

JRD : I think 20 July 1980, when my wife got a stroke and
she spent a month or two in hospital. . . .
When I played golf I used to run off immediately after lunch
every holiday. And every other day of the week I was in the
office, so I never was with Thelly. Then I spent weekends
with her. When she became seriously ill, I thought she could
die anytime and so I gave up golf; but she (has) survived
for seven years and two months after her stroke.** I never
started playing again.'

● ● ●

* He related that once in an unguarded moment the paper he was
  dictating from was blown off from under the desk by a gust of wind,
  and Iyer happened to pick it up to JRD's mortification!
** The interview took place on 24 September 1987. Thelly Tata survived
   J.R.D. Tata by ten months.

He was convinced, having read some books on the subject, that compared to the life-span of animals the body of man was meant to function till the age of 120. He said that we did not live that long because we did not exercise enough. He was a great one for exercise. In his early years he worked out with dumb-bells because he was extremely thin, though wiry and strong.

RML : You were very skinny, weren't you, in your youth?

JRD : Very skinny. I had a thin skin too.

RML : Do you do deep breathing exercises at all?

JRD : I don't believe in slow exercises. I know they're wonderful. I don't contest that but I don't enjoy, or like or believe in slow exercises. I believe in putting maximum strain on the muscle. You then automatically go into deep breathing because you get out of breath. When you do deep knee-bends or things like that you get out of breath. So I don't bother to do separate deep breathing exercises. It comes naturally.

He admitted that when he gave up skiing in 1987 he lost his motivation to keep his muscles toned. And when muscles that have been exercised for years are suddenly neglected they sag badly, especially when one is in his eighties. In his last years he had difficulty walking. He fell down a couple of times and it was a miracle he did not break any bones. A friend of his said that a skilled skier is trained how to fall with the least injury and he knew how to fall.

I had the privilege of travelling with him on his last flight within India to Hyderabad and back in July 1993. Those who knew him well were conscious that he did not like anybody supporting him even when he was shaky on his feet. What he did welcome was the offer of a forearm which he would hold on to to steady himself.

As we were going through the air bridge into the plane, there was a small step to be negotiated. He stumbled badly and was almost heading for the floor. An Indian Airlines official quickly held him, with me following. JRD shook off the two hands which came to his rescue so vigorously and said so angrily, 'Don't hold me,' that even I was taken aback. The airline official who had helped him was quite upset.

I observed to JRD: 'You know, Sir, you could have fallen down!'

'Never mind,' he said defiantly and walked on. At other times when people tried to hold him he would react and say 'What do you think? Am I a cripple?'

In spite of the pleadings of his colleagues who cared for him, he refused to use a walking stick.

● ● ●

ON SKIING AND AGE

RML : You started skiing late in life, didn't you?

JRD : I started, alas, only in 1946, after the war. I was forty-two, much too old. It's entirely a sport for the young and if possible the youngest. They put them on skis at the age of two or three now. They ski quite fast for little things. By the time a boy or girl is three or four they're afraid of nothing and you see them coming down in droves. It's a lovely sight. Usually people stop skiing by the time they're forty.

RML : But you skiied much faster in your younger days.

JRD : No, same speed. I skiied faster in my sixties because by then I had developed the skills. It's not a natural thing to be on skis. Yes, if you've been on skates and ice, you're all right. Or if you've done a lot of roller skating then you get the balance. The body's not used to travelling fast on wheels or on ice or on skis.

RML : Where do you normally ski?

JRD : From Geneva I go to wherever we decide to go. This will be the third season I'll go to Austria to start with. For the last two seasons, after fifteen days in Austria we (Robert Robins and himself) went down to the Dolomites in Italy, the upper part of Italy, which is all part of the same Alps.

RML : How do you spend time during your holidays? Do you ski in the morning or in the afternoon?

JRD : I don't ski early in the morning anymore. The youngsters, those who are fanatics and healthy and young, they want to ski all day so they go up by the first funicular or whatever transportation is provided. By 8 a.m. the first group are out there. Then by about 12 o'clock everybody gets off the main slope and goes to various restaurants. At every station there are restaurants which get very full but that is the time when the slopes are idle and I don't want to ski much more than two or three hours. So I go late, I go about 11.30-12 o'clock when the cable cars are much freer and then I ski for as long as possible and then we have a very late sandwich somewhere and then ski down. I ski for a total of perhaps three hours. Not continuous, when I come down the slope I stop at corners. I admire the view—take it easy . . . .

RML : How do you keep your body in trim the rest of the year?

JRD : By exercise for the legs—for instance, skiing is for the legs. I've got a bicycle which I use everyday, for two minutes at a time. Then for the rest of the body I do deep knee bends, also push ups. My favourite exercise for the chest and for the arms is done with my legs up on the bath tub.

I've got a plank, a padded plank which unfortunately I don't use now. It is an ideal exercise device for the stomach, and helps to prevent stomach growth, keeping the muscles strong, because these muscles are loose. The padded plank has a strap at one end for your feet to be put in and then you just lean it against the wall. I've got straps on the wall (in his exercise room) at various levels, so you can adjust the height. Then you sit on it with your feet up and you can stay, if you want, in that position for as long as you like, hanging from there. What I do is strap my feet in, with my hands behind my head, and then rise about ten times. That is the maximum. A lot of people just do it on the floor. You put your feet under a seat and then you sit up—but when you sit there, there is no strain. But if your feet are up in the air at the maximum angle, then there is maximum contraction of the muscles. That exercise is something I should continue to do, but it's a nuisance. You've got to put the damn thing there, then sit on it, get your feet up underneath. I'm lazy. But I should do it because that's the only way to keep this (pointing to his stomach) down.

He demonstrated this exercise to me, strapping his feet to the padded board, keeping his head down, body at a forty-five degree angle, hands behind his head. Once in position, he rose against gravity, once, twice, thrice, at great speed. He was red in the face. I cried out, 'Enough, Sir,' fearing he would get a heart attack.

In 1987, I enquired if he had his heart checked regularly.

JRD : Not regularly, I do it every four or five years.

RML : Four or five years!!!

JRD : I've done it three times in the last ten years.

RML : You come out, touch wood, with flying colours—do you?

JRD : No. The first time it was not so bad, then the next time they said it was less good, and the last time it was better. Also, I am careful when I ski. When you ski or do any exercise, your heartbeat begins to grow and you must sense how far you can go. I don't hesitate, if I'm out of breath and I can feel my heart thumping—I stop. I let my heart rate go down and only then do I get going again. So, if you control yourself like that you're not likely to hurt yourself. When you're young you try to do the maximum you can—you can hurt yourself.

RML : Apart from concerns about your physical fitness, I reckon you probably have a very good temperament. You've kept yourself cheerful.

JRD : I'll tell you there is another thing that keeps me going. I mean beyond the things you can regulate yourself, like eating, drinking, smoking. I'm surprised it's not used more often. I am talking about hormones—the male hormone for the men and female hormone for the women. One of the well-known things that everybody knows or should know, is that as you get older the output of those hormones goes down. And it is obvious that when that happens they have to be replaced. This procedure is called HRT—Hormone Replacement Therapy. You take injections every ten-fifteen days or whatever the doctors advise. For women and men there is a danger only in that you've got to watch out that it doesn't have any side-effects. *

All men after a certain age have prostate growth. The thing to do is to take it out, not to wait too long, because it is an irreversible condition. If you take hormones in excessive quantity or too early, one of the effects of the male hormones is to make your prostate grow faster—it's OK but in any case you've got to have it out sooner or later. How many people get cancer (of the prostate) because they just wait too long and they don't have it out? Since I'd given some thought to this, I decided that from the age of fifty I would get my doctor to give me regular hormone therapy. I've been doing that now for the last thirty years—in fact forty years. Since after the war, since the forties when Jal Patel was my doctor. So I've been on male hormones all these years.

In 1987, when the cable car he was taking to the ski slopes took a turn, he fell and had a hairline fracture of the hip. He said to me, 'It was a silly accident. I was not attentive.' After that he decided that it was time to call it a day where skiing was concerned.

---

* His late doctor Gool Contractor told me of the dangers of this therapy. A company director who took higher doses than he should have, died of cancer of the liver.

PERSONAL PREFERENCES

As a young man, on his visits to Europe, JRD took in motor racing events and tennis championships. He said: 'I would have liked to be a motor racer. I have liked everything that was a little on the edge, on the verge of disaster. Living dangerously.' Once, in the 1920s, in his racing Bugatti, he covered the distance from Worli to Kirkee in two hours and thirteen minutes.

He was an occasional visitor to natural history museums, but he did not visit art galleries or the great western museums because he thought he would be able to study the works of the geniuses of art better in art books. A taste for art developed later in life, but he was always interested in music.

● ● ●

MUSIC

RML : Disraeli found expression in his novels. Perhaps, had you continued your music which you stopped at a fairly young age . . . .

JRD : By that time my mother was very ill and we were

moving about. To play the piano well, you've got to remain in one place. You can always get a piano teacher but normally you want a piano in the house, you want to practice, you want to stay in the same place and I didn't think I had the talent. No—I might have had, because I had a very accurate ear and I could have done something with it. Maybe in my next life.

He once mentioned that after he had settled down in life he could have still developed a taste for music. 'But,' he said, 'it is time-consuming and in any case Thelly was not that interested.'

On one occasion, when a group of youngsters accompanied by a guitarist came to sing to him at his office he politely told the guitarist to play softly as he was drowning out the voices of the singers.

● ● ●

FOOD HABITS

RML : Tell me a little about your food habits.

JRD : Always sober. I'm sorry to say—maybe that's the way I've kept in shape—I don't particularly enjoy food. Food is something to eat and I usually don't know what I'm eating or what I've eaten. If you were to ask me what I've had to eat for lunch, I wouldn't know. Unless I make an effort. It's a pity, because according to many of my friends trying food is great—it's one of the joys of life, which it's never been to me. My food habits are totally uninteresting.

This probably applied to his food habits at home or to lunches at Bombay House. When he went out to eat, JRD could be choosy and critical about food and showed a weakness for prawns. Invariably, they were his first choice. A man of considerable discipline, his weakness for prawns (the primary cause of his occasional stomach upsets) was surprising.

● ● ●

WINES

The first recipient of the Daniel Guggenheim Award was Orville Wright. In 1988, JRD was given this award at a function at the Boeing plant in Seattle. Red and white wine from choice vineyards was specially bottled, with JRD's sketch on the bottle, saying that this wine was bottled on the occasion of the award to J.R.D. Tata.

RML : What about wines? You seem to be a connoisseur of wines, though you don't drink too much.

JRD : I never was a connoisseur because to be a connoisseur you've got to live in a country that has wine. Anyway, India's not the place, except at a very high cost, to judge any wine and the wine that comes is not much good. But abroad, at every meal in a restaurant, I always have wine. If I'm with friends and if I want a young gay wine, just a nice wine, then I ask the advice of the wine waiters who know their wine. In this way, I've learnt a fair amount. Wine is an annual thing. You may have one year that was good for a particular vineyard or area of France, for instance. The next year it isn't good. So you've got to know the vintage. I like wine, I like to know about it. I'm interested.

RML : You don't like anything stronger? Have you never been addicted to stronger liquor?

JRD : No, I don't even like the taste.

Though drink never affected JRD—save once, when he drove his car home with difficulty—he said his attitude to alcoholics changed from a hasty critical judgement to a more compassionate one thanks to Jehangir B. Patel. They were on a voyage together in the 1930s and one of the passengers was a drunkard. J. B. Patel took him in hand and explained, 'Jeh, he is a sick man. He needs help.'

●　●　●

SMOKING

RML : Did you smoke cigars when you were younger?

JRD : Never, I tried to smoke a pipe in England when I was a youngster. It kept my hands warm. Otherwise, no.

RML : So you never took to smoking or drinking?

JRD : Yes, smoking, I used to smoke cigarettes. Quite heavily until 31 December 1967.

RML : How did you give it up?

JRD : By deciding long before to give it up and then doing it by degrees. I decided I'd take two or three years but you've got to have an emotional build-up. The build-up to say, 'All right, I'll give it up on the 31st.' You've got to give it up on the 31st, as you've got to give up something on 31st December. Amongst Europeans, you give up something. I said, 'All right, I don't gamble, I don't drink, I smoke, I don't womanize more than others. So the easiest thing is to give up smoking.'

RML : And you did—you've never touched it since?

JRD : Yes. On the 31st of December 1967, I smoked like a chimney till midnight and then gave it up. So that was the end of it and I never smoked again.

● ● ●

WOMEN

At a meeting at Sydenham College, when a young man asked him about his colourful youth, JRD replied,'It was not colourful as made out. As a young man I was shy about women but I am no longer shy now—but what is the use *now!*'

He later told me, 'I have got an exaggerated reputation of a Casanova whom women run after and I have tried to encourage it. The company of women does give me great pleasure and at any party unless there is a man who is outstanding or whom I want to meet, I prefer to go to the company of women. Young and old respond to me. Men usually talk about business or tell silly jokes or get drunk. You know, I find complimenting women makes a great difference. If a lady is dressed well, you mention that. Sometimes I see a lady after a long time and I say, "You have changed your hairdo." It is a bit of a pleasant fraud. I have the pleasure of giving pleasure and it gives me pleasure too.'

He spoke of compatibility between couples; he spoke of physical compatibility. He felt that if people could live with each other a while before marriage they would know each other's idiosyncrasies better. 'Sometimes even different habits can be quite devastating in a marriage.'

He then spoke of being an admirer of beauty and the human form, both male and female. While sensitive to the physical aspect, he said what meant most to him was the aesthetic value as in the Ice Ballet he saw in Bombay and the figures of the ladies.

But he did say to me that although his reputation as a playboy was an exaggeration, he had not lived as the Bible wanted him to live.

●   ●   ●

SLEEP

RML : When did you normally get up when you were at your physical peak?

JRD : Same time, about seven-thirty. Sometimes when I find that I cannot sleep, the choice is between taking a pill or reading something and then going back to bed. I prefer to read and go back to sleep than to lie awake.

RML : Are you a light sleeper?

JRD : Yes—I used to be a fairly light sleeper. I used to admire Nowroji Saklatvala (JRD's predecessor as Chairman of Tata Sons) who used to say that he could never remember when he went to bed. Because he (Sir Nowroji) said the moment he put his head on the pillow, he went to sleep—lucky man. I think Jawaharlal Nehru was like that. Some people can sleep on a gun carriage!! Ratan Tata, I'm glad for him, can sleep on a plane. I can't sleep—very little on a plane, unless I drug myself.

RML : So you get up about seven-thirty, then you read the papers?

JRD : I read the papers—I read a number of papers so it takes about forty to forty-five minutes—then at eight-fifteen, breakfast. I never could get up like the Hindus and others and be at the golf course at dawn. I tried that once or twice— I just couldn't wake up.

RML : When do you do your exercise?

JRD : In the evening, after work.

INDIA

JRD was born five thousand miles away from India, but I have met few Indians who loved their country as deeply. Unlike most of us who have hardened ourselves to the poverty, shoddiness and callousness around us, he remained deeply sensitive to the needs of the country and his countrymen.

Once, when we were waiting for a flight to take off in 1993, I asked: 'You are a precise, time-conscious, methodical person who likes everything neat and clean. You must at times find yourself an alien in India, as I sometimes do.'

It seemed to be a new thought to him. He hesitated. Then he said, 'I suppose so.'

More than once when he talked of reincarnation he would say: 'I tell people I would like to come to India and part of me wants to return because India is such an interesting country.' But then he would stop and add that he could not once again 'go through the pain of witnessing the conditions and poverty of our people.' It was this feeling that prompted him to think of social responsibilities of companies beyond their concern for their staff and workers. As mentioned earlier, in 1969, at an important speech in Madras he spoke of industry adopting the villages in its neighbourhood and sparing its managers, its engineers, doctors and skilled specialists to help, advise and 'supervise new developments undertaken by co-operative effort between them and the company. Assistance in family planning in the villages would be a particularly valuable form of service.'

His companies in Jamshedpur quickly pursued his ideas through rural development work and others followed suit. Thousands of villagers have acquired skills and employment. If today a Santhal tribal woman in the forests near Jamshedpur is earning a livelihood, it is because in faraway Bombay a senior man, whose name she may never have heard and whose face she may never have seen, thought of the needs of people like herself, his companies helping her and her neighbours learn a trade and find markets for the goods they produce. TISCO alone gives this facility to 250 villages, with TELCO, Tata Chemicals and other companies following its lead. By awakening industry to social responsibility, JRD gave to industry a soul and a purpose beyond profit.

● ● ●

PERSONALITIES OF THE FREEDOM STRUGGLE

In the Foreword to his book *Keynote,** JRD speaks about the personalities of the freedom struggle whom he knew, some better than others. He had not met Gandhi too often (four or five times only) and did not claim to know him too well. He knew Nehru much better. It was a peculiar relationship

---

* See appendix.

in later years in so far as although they both had a personal respect and affection for each other, their thinking was poles apart and Nehru tried to avoid any discussion on the economy with JRD. 'He always looked out of the window or asked me to look at the panda in his garden whenever I wanted to talk seriously about the economy.'

JRD retained his affection for Nehru till the end but this was mixed with sadness because he knew the relationship could never fully blossom. In his letter to me on my chapter on Nehru and himself he wrote: 'Sharing as I did Jawaharlal's deep sympathy for the poor and deep urge to alleviate their poverty, I was denied, or denied myself, opportunities to help him in that task by my disagreement with his socialism.' The words 'denied myself' are significant.

The person he was most fond of was J.P. Narayan. He wrote of him in *Keynote* that he had met him in connection with a labour problem at Jamshedpur and was 'impressed by his transparent sincerity and gentlemanly reasonableness, unexpected in an ex-revolutionary activist. It was, in fact, this unreasonable reasonableness, which I believe prevented him from being an effective political leader and playing the powerful part that he could have played in Indian politics.' JRD then mentioned a couple of JP's traits : 'He was too honest and too prone to see the other side and would never be a party to the political shenanigans into which Indian politics increasingly sank.' It is interesting that JRD should point this out because JRD himself, like JP, was too honest and too prone to see the other side and to accept compromises through consensus except on matters of ethical business practice. JP reflected his own nature and hence the bond between the two men. He also shared JP's ability to respect the other person's point of view, even if he did not agree with it. JRD would disagree without being disagreeable and seldom forced his views from the authority of his position.

He was obviously fond of Sarojini Naidu. She was, he said, 'A poetess with a great sense of humour and gaiety. She gave you confidence by her ability to laugh, which incidentally Gandhiji also had.'

In his personal scrapbook he had copied down a beautiful poem by Sarojini Naidu:

*You held a wild flower in your finger tips,
Idly you pressed it to your indifferent lips,
Idly you tore its crimson leaves apart.
Alas! it was my heart.*

*You held a wine cup in your finger tips,
Lightly you raised it to indifferent lips,
Lightly you drank and flung away the bowl,
Alas! it was my soul.*

● ● ●

'WOULD I HAVE ACCEPTED A MINISTERSHIP?'

'If you did not accept Nehru's invitation to be on the U.N. delegation for the second year running, in 1949,' I enquired, 'would you have accepted, say, in 1948/49, when things were good, a ministership in Industry or Finance?'

'Oh yes,' JRD heartily replied, 'I would have for Aviation (too). But one thing I would not have done. I would not have accepted an Ambassadorship—except Switzerland.' The interview took place at a time when Bofors was in the news and the Swiss accounts of various people were being looked into by the Government. So I enquired : 'To

'No, because I would have been able to ski there three months of the year!' he replied.
He went on to say that even as Minister, say, of Industries, he didn't think he could have lasted for long. Nehru with his 'socialism and licences' would not have fitted in with his thinking.

•   •   •

APPROACH TO THE PUBLIC SECTOR

It is a measure of his wanting the best for India that in the late 1950s and early 1960s JRD gave full support to the Government in erecting factories for steel of which, till then, Tatas were the main producers. People who had qualified at Tatas supplied many of the skills to the newborn steel plants. 'My quarrel with Nehru was not that he wanted to put up steel plants,' JRD told me. 'My quarrel was that they did not think big enough and wanted to put up small steel plants with small capacities.' JRD wanted the public and private sector to walk arm in arm.

Just after JRD completed twenty-five years as Chairman of Tata Sons, *The Economic and Political Weekly* wrote on 3 August 1963:

> The Silver Jubilee of JRD Tata as the Head of the Tata Group of Companies (25 July) was not accompanied by any great fanfare. Regardless of how others took the occasion, Shri JRD Tata himself has celebrated it in his own characteristic manner. He has looked

forward, not back. Witness his firm support to the Bokaro (Steel) project in the public sector on the ground that 'it would be both unreasonable and unpatriotic of anyone to place the interests of private enterprise above those of the nation as a whole.' The man who was born into the family of India's greatest captain of industry, made it clear that 'the private sector, even if permitted to do so, would not be able to undertake on its own a programme of expansion at an average rate exceeding a million tons of new capacity per year.'

From 1953 to 1978, JRD was in a unique position to weigh the merits and demerits of the private sector and the public sector as he was the head of one of the largest public sector companies—Air India—as well as the chief of some of the largest private companies in the country like TISCO and TELCO. He saw no conflict between the two sectors, each of which complemented the other. What he did object to was the disproportionate role allocated to the public sector in fields where the private sector could operate just as well or with greater efficiency. He observed that the initiative and even decision-making by responsible heads of the public sector was stifled by senior bureaucrats and ministers.

When he spoke of Air India, he often mentioned how he kept the bureaucrats in the Ministry at bay and how they often tried to push their weight around. * He was the only public sector head with the stature to put bureaucrats in their place.

---

* He once related to me how Krishna Menon tried to foist on Air India a senior official of the Indian Air Force who was a 'bounder' as Managing Director and how he (JRD) stood up to the person who then was the most powerful Minister after the Prime Minister—and won his point.

who said: 'The history of liberty is the history of the limitations
of the governmental power, not the increase of it.'

●　　●　　●

FOR BUREAUCRATS AND JUDGES

For almost two decades JRD felt strongly about the low
salaries of judges and bureaucrats. He occasionally mentioned
this to the powers that be in Delhi, with little effect.

Just before Indira Gandhi came back to power in 1980,
a respected civil servant, known for his integrity, requested
a Tata director to see whether Tatas could fill petrol in his
car on their account because he could not afford it on his
salary. He needed the petrol to send his children to school.
It brought home to JRD the situation facing honest officials
who wield considerable power and had access to, if they
wished, millions of rupees.

JRD had his Economics and Statistics Department work
out for him the salaries of ICS officers and judges in British
times (Rs.4,000 per month in those days) and compared it
with salaries in the late 1970s, which, given the cost of living,
amounted to a staggering cut in income. Armed with the
facts, he met Indira Gandhi, the then Prime Minister. 'I told
her that the business of the salary of judges and senior civil
servants was getting ridiculous and their salary, far from
keeping pace with inflation, was getting eroded and
reduced. Even several directors of Air India and Indian
Airlines were getting a ridiculous sum of Rs 3,500.'

Indira Gandhi during her last term of office did bring about a rise in salaries—though not as fairly as JRD had hoped for.

When I told JRD that this was an important contribution he had made, especially as other top industrialists were equally aware of the problem but had done nothing about it, he brushed it aside. 'We were not the only ones who realized that. In fact, some others* realized it only too well— and earlier than Tatas—but they found it more helpful for their business to get things done (by making civil servants dependent on them) than to set right an injustice.'

● ● ●

INDIA'S FUTURE

At a Rotary Club meeting in 1991 he was asked what he saw for the future. He said: 'I am an old man now, one always hopes one can live a little longer. I would like young people to think about serious questions facing the country. We are an extraordinary and capable people with a long history. In the short run one may not be an optimist but in the long run I do see a future for India.'

● ● ●

LOOKING FORWARD TO THE 21ST CENTURY

Speaking in January 1986 to Sharoukh Sabavala and myself, he mentioned with regret that no Prime Minister of India

---

* He spoke as if he had one or two specifically in mind and it was not a sweeping statement as his words seem to indicate.

had really used his services except through Air India which
was his own baby. 'Although eighty years old, I still feel I
can do something (for the country and through the
Government).' He mentioned that Nehru did not trust
business people, nor did Indira; and though he felt Rajiv
was not distrustful of him, it had never crossed his mind to
use his services. 'In other countries the skills of top people
in industry are utilized at least for a year or two by the
Government.'

He later observed: 'I would like to see the turn of the
century.'

Mr Sabavala and I said that he probably would still be
around at ninety-six but were not sure we would be!

JRD said: 'It really won't be any different from the
twentieth but one thing that excites me is the thought of
supersonic planes which will go directly into the
stratosphere where there is no friction and then descend at
the other end, which would mean that the flight across the
Atlantic will be of one hour!'

●   ●   ●

'WHAT I WANT INDIA TO BE'

One of the most moving occasions I have been to was the
function, in 1992, to honour JRD on being awarded the
Bharat Ratna. It was a strictly Tata staff occasion where
even spouses were not invited. Two thousand people turned
up. It was held on the grounds of the NCPA in Bombay.
Jamshed Bhabha, the creator of the NCPA, had made

meticulous arrangements, including an invitation to a choir called 'Stopgaps'. Just a few speakers paid tribute to JRD. And he was thoroughly at home speaking to his own family members. He said he could speak freely to them. 'You are my friends,' he paused and affectionately added, 'you are my *children.*' At this point many eyes were wet. It was a wide ranging speech. He spoke about Tatas and the country. He said, 'The one thing that has made life worthwhile for me is the feeling of being esteemed. Being loved is a great feeling.' He said that the years that might remain of him 'would be devoted to basking in the glory of the affection and respect I have received.' Mr Ratan Tata mentioned that when advance word reached him about JRD being chosen for the Bharat Ratna and he mentioned it to JRD, his first reaction was : 'Can't we do something to stop it!'

At the end of the function, after quite a few had departed, JRD shook hands with scores of people and made his way towards the choir which had not dispersed. As he approached, the choir leader, Alfred D'Souza, led the singers into a rendition of 'Edelweis' from the *Sound of Music*. It was touching to see the grand old man facing the choir, keeping tune with the song which goes:

Edelweis, Edelweis, every morning you greet me
Edelweis, small and white
You look happy to meet me
Long may you bloom and grow
Bloom and grow forever
Edelweis, Edelweis, bless my homeland forever.

MISCELLANEOUS

DEMISE OF COMMUNISM

Twice, to my knowledge, JRD foresaw the collapse of Communism. In October 1987, JRD was weighing, as he occasionally did, where he would like to be born in his next life. In the course of it he said, 'Switzerland and Germany will be dull , peaceful, clean and neat and maybe I would like that. I'd rather be in Italy or France . . . but China?' he asked himself but did not answer. I inquired : 'Not Russia?' JRD replied, 'When I come back Russia may be a completely different society. Not too big—it is huge. To me a society of that size becomes unmanageable.' In 1987, the Soviet Empire was a powerful monolith from Minsk to Vladivostok. Only two years after our conversation it started splitting with the collapse of the Berlin Wall.

JRD had read history and was fond of it and was convinced that one day Communism would collapse. In a letter to J.P. Narayan on 4 January 1955 he wrote:

> I must confess that I do not share your understanding of the capitalist system or its place in history. With great respect, I wonder whether you are not making the mistake of viewing the capitalist system as it was many years ago and not as it is today or in the form

into which it is clearly developing all over the world. It is true that such evolution is somewhat uneven and that progress has been less in economically backward countries such as ours than in the more advanced democracies of the West, but the trend is clear and unmistakeable and I am convinced that those who are today so confident in sealing the fate of the capitalist system on behalf of history are likely to change their mind in due course or to regret the change which they will have brought about. I believe that in most parts of the world the system of free enterprise, far from dying, will be given a renewed lease of life in recognition of its ability and willingness to serve the community well and also from a revulsion against the unpleasant reality—as distinct from the myth—of State Socialism.

J.P. Narayan did not live to see these words come true thirty-five years later with the historic reversal of East Europe to an economy of free enterprise. But JP did forsake Marxism a few years later, stating that Marxism provided 'no incentive to goodness in man'.

JRD lived to see his prophecy come true. In March 1991, when I showed him his words to J.P., he read them aloud carefully, the last lines twice over. 'Not too bad,' he said. Without claiming any credit he returned the paper to me.

A few months later when I finished my biography of him he spoke of his love for history—Greek, Roman and Napoleonic. He believed it was that perspective which enabled him to read the trends of his time. Then he inquired what I would write after this book. 'You should write on the 'Death of a Religion' he said, repeating the words. I was perplexed till he added, firmly, 'Communism.' He observed that when he was at school in Paris, 'Communism was a religion to my Marxist teachers'. And asked, 'Where is it now?'

• • •

ON KISSINGER

I inquired about the international personalities he had met and admired. The first one he mentioned was Edgar Faure, former Speaker of the French Parliament who had held a number of ministerial posts. 'A highly civilized and educated man.'

Another man he mentioned was the famous post-war Prime Minister of France, Leon Blum. Nehru took him along to translate for him but 'with the little French Nehru knew and the little English that Blum knew, they got along pretty well.'

André Malraux, author and French Minister for Culture, was the next. 'A remarkable man, an agitated type, a prestigious man who transformed Paris, who had the public buildings cleaned. First he wrote in simple ways, but then he began to philosophize.'

He knew President Valery Giscard d'Estaing, but he knew Prime Minister Jacques Chirac better. Chirac reported to him at length on his visit to China, hoping JRD would be able to influence Mrs Gandhi on Indo-Chinese relations.

David Rockefeller, then the head of the Chase Manhattan Bank, organized an International Advisory Council of the Bank which would not discuss details of banking work but would take a view of the developments on the world economic scene. It met in different countries every six months. The Advisory Council would meet in different parts of the world, often in New York. The Council consisted of twenty-six of the top industrialists and business tycoons of the world and usually one or two representatives from selected countries. As an exception Henry Kissinger was regularly invited. He usually presented an overview of major world trends and different industrialists from different countries would talk of developments in their region. JRD found these meetings most stimulating and was somewhat proud that he was a member of this body for a couple of decades. JRD stepped down from the Advisory Council at the same time as he stepped down from the Chairmanship of Tata Sons in 1991.

At the Advisory Council Henry Kissinger became a good friend of his and so did David Rockefeller, 'a fine citizen'. JRD had also met Nelson Rockefeller when he was Assistant Secretary of State in the 1950s and JRD needed some help with modernization of Tata Steel. He was surprised that when he met Rockefeller twenty years later, when the latter was Governor of New York, he remembered in detail what JRD had met him about. JRD always respected a good memory, especially as he had a phenomenal one himself. On Kissinger, he said : 'What I like about Henry Kissinger is his sense of humour. He is always making cracks about himself. He is not pompous at all. Kissinger explains in his two books why he sent the 7th Fleet in—because of the advice he got that India having defeated Pakistan in Bengal would then turn around and demolish it in the West. And I told him later that that was a very wrong judgement on his part. Then it became clear from his book that what he was concerned with at the time was his approach to China and he had to prepare Nixon's visit to China, which was an enormous event in connection with the Russians; and the way to go to China was through Pakistan. His secret

President R. Venkataraman conferring the Bharat Ratna, March 1992

At a reception at the Indian Institute of Science, March 1992

Rajiv Gandhi awarding J. R. D. Tata the Gold Air Medal from the Federation Aeronautique Internationale, 1985

At the U. N. Population Award ceremony 1992, with Boutrous Boutrous-Ghali, U. N. Secretary-General on his left

Speaking at the Museum of Flight, U.S.A. after receiving the
Daniel Guggenheim Medal Award, 1988

In a reflective moment

Photo: Courtesy Jehangir Nicholson

JRD at a reception given by the Parsi Panchayat

I have a Rendezvous with Death......

I have a rendezvous with Death
At some disputed barricade,
When Spring comes back with rustling shade
And apple-blossoms fill the air—
I have a rendezvous with Death
When Spring brings back blue days and fair.

It may be he shall take my hand
And lead me into his dark land
And close my eyes and quench my breath—
It may be I shall pass him still.
I have a rendezvous with Death
On some scarred slope of battered hill,
When Spring comes round again this year
And the first meadow-flies appear.

God knows 'twere better to be deep
Pillowed in silk and scented down,
Where Love throbs out in blissfull sleep,
Pulse nigh to pulse, and breath to breath,
Where hushed awakenings are dear......

But I've a rendezvous with Death
At midnight in some flaming town,
When Spring trips north again this year,
And I to my pledged word am true,
I shall not fail that rendezvous.

Last Poems (1915)   ALAN SEEGER

From the personal scrapbook of J. R. D. Tata, in his own handwriting

Dr. Shankar Dayal Sharma releasing the Stamp Album of J. R. D. Tata flanked by Sukh Ram, Minister of State for Communications and Ratan Tata

trip to China was through Pakistan and back and that is why he felt that if we went and attacked Pakistan it would be impossible for him to execute his policy on China. When he came to India after JRD died, Dr Kissinger told me he first met JRD in 1978. In 1987 JRD came up to him and said: 'Henry, you know you are not very popular in India, but I would like you to come and deliver the Sir Dorab Tata Memorial Lecture.' Dr Kissinger could not come then but when he did finally come in March 1995, this time at the invitation of Mr R.N. Tata, he made a very moving reference to JRD at the beginning of his lecture at the Tata Theatre:

> It is a great honour for me to speak on this occasion and my only regret is that Jeh Tata could not be here. I have met many remarkable men in my life. I have not met anyone more distinguished, more remarkable than Jeh Tata. And perhaps one of the reasons why my visit was always delayed was the conviction all of us carried with us that he was indestructible.

● ● ●

MOTHER TERESA AND JRD

In September 1990, Sharoukh Sabavala related the following incident to me:

> When Mother Teresa visited Jamshedpur she was flown back in the private plane of Tata Steel to Calcutta. Accompanying her in the aircraft were J.R.D. Tata, Russi Mody and Sabavala. The sun was setting on the horizon and Mother Teresa took out

her rosary to say her evening prayer. That did not dampen the enthusiasm of JRD who kept interrupting her, speaking generally about the poverty of India and how it upset him and when would it end, and so on. Sabavala was trying to whisper to him amidst the drone of the aeroplane's engines : 'She is praying, she is praying.' Finally, Mother Teresa raised her head and said : 'Mr Tata, why are you worrying about poverty? Your work is to open more industries, give more employment to people and leave the rest to God!

Mr Sabavala added that there was no further interruption of the Mother's prayers till journey's end half an hour later.

● ● ●

BHARAT RATNA—1992

It was the measure of the man, who was awarded India's highest civilian award—the Bharat Ratna (Jewel of India)—that the citation he valued the most was the comparatively obscure Dadabhai Naoroji Award of Rs 10,000! He had read with admiration about Dadabhai Naoroji knocking on doors of Bombay homes in the 1880s, requesting fathers to send their daughters to school. This Award gave him the direction and the thrust that his new Trust—the J.R.D. and Thelma J. Tata Trust—was to take. He put most of the sale proceeds of his flat (a few crore rupees) into this Trust.

The U.N. Population Award, which was bestowed on him in New York eight months after he received the Bharat Ratna, was the last of the many awards showered upon him. The others were: The Padma Vibhushan, 1955; Knight Commander of the Order of St. Gregory the Great (Papal

Honour), 1964; Knight Commander's Cross of the Order of Merit of the Federal Republic of Germany, 1978; Tony Jannus Award, 1979; Commander of the Legion of Honour of the French Government, 1983; Gold Air Medal of the Federation Aeronautique Internationale, 1985; Bessemer Medal of the Institute of Metals, London, 1986; Edward Warner Award by the International Civil Aviation Organisation, 1986; and Daniel Guggenheim Award, 1988.

He was a shy man for almost all his life. In 1981, when Ratan Tata was made Chairman of Tata Industries, both he and Ratan came in for a lot of publicity. After giving a few interviews he suddenly withdrew into his shell. At the time, he said to me: 'I am over-exposed.' But when the Bharat Ratna was given to him nine years later, he decided to enjoy the publicity, almost to the point of making up for the years of shying away from the glare of publicity.

We were once going out to lunch at the Nehru Centre's 'Jewel of India' restaurant. I mentioned to him that I was then staying with my hostess, Mrs Jini Talyerkhan. 'Invite her too,' he said. 'Tell her the Jewel of India invites you to lunch at the Jewel of India!'

For a few days after getting the award he kept saying, 'I don't deserve it.' So I sent him Jack Benny's comment which amused him. Jack Benny had said : 'I don't deserve this award, but I've arthritis and I don't deserve that either.'

III

FAST FALLS THE EVENTIDE

ON AGE
ON DEATH
BEYOND DEATH
ON GOD AND RELIGION
ON PRAYER
MEETING WITH FATHER BALAGUER

FAST FALLS THE EVENTIDE

The Muse of History must not be fastidious. She must see everything, touch everything, and, if possible, smell everything. She need not be afraid that these intimate details will rob her of Romance and Hero-worship. Recorded trifles and tittle-tattle may—and indeed ought to—wipe out small people. They can have no permanent effect upon those who held with honour the foremost stations in the greatest storms.

—Winston S. Churchill, *Great Contemporaries*

ON AGE

When I saw JRD on the eve of his eighty-sixth or eighty-seventh birthday, I showed him a passage from the 'Treasury of Joy and Enthusiasm' by Norman Vincent Peale. It was a passage that echoed his own feelings. Peale quoted Sir William Mulock, Chief Justice of Ontario, who on his ninety-fifth birthday said: 'The shadows of evening lengthen about me, but morning is in my heart.' Justice Mulock added, 'The Castle of Enchantment is not yet behind me. It is before me still, and daily I catch a glimpse of its battlements and towers. The rich sports of memory are mine. The best of all is friends. Mine, too, are the precious things of today—books, flowers, pictures, nature and sport .... The best of life is always further on.'

Justice William Mulock was credited with having '(an) unfailing childlike appetite for what's next and joy in the game of life.' JRD had that attitude. Like Victor Hugo, JRD could well have said, 'Winter is on my head, but spring is in my heart.' Of course, the length of age is not the only criterion for a life well lived; as Seneca said, 'Let us see to it . . . that our lives, like jewels of great price, be noteworthy not because of their width, but because of their weight.' JRD's width of life was considerable, and there was weight to it too. He lived a full life almost upto his eighty-ninth birthday and only in the last four months did he lose his zest for life.

Minoo Masani recalls that in the 1950s, when he worked for Tatas, JRD would react to even being wished on his birthday. If anybody mentioned it, he would be snubbed. 'At the same time,' says an old colleague, A. K. Banerjee, 'he didn't like it forgotten either.' In 1988 Masani told me, 'Now Jeh has mellowed. He doesn't bristle when honoured or wished. In the old days you would dare not wish him on his birthday without his coming back, "You too".' I am told that instead of 29 July, the festive spirit invaded JRD's circle on the 30th and he was all smiles then and sometimes even apologetic for his behaviour—'I didn't mean it,' he would say.

On his eighty-third birthday, when I went to see him before lunch, he was warm. I found twelve baskets of red roses lining the tops of bookshelves in his anteroom, with two baskets of yellow roses standing out in the centre. When I commented on them he said, 'O but the ones that came home this morning have already been sent to the hospital.'

'You know,' he said, 'I disliked my birthdays.' He then

went on to reveal why : 'I was very shy and felt I could not return the presents.'

• • •

ON DEATH

When we met on 9 August 1987, we talked about death.

JRD : I am not terribly worried about death. I would probably be smart enough to die when I am abroad. I want to make sure that I am not a nuisance to anyone. Can you imagine, if I die in France—will people come there?

RML : But you have done so much for people.

JRD : But I don't think people being around will serve any useful purpose. I would like to die somewhere on my travels, in an air-crash or disappear in the sea. At least to die in a way that I am not a nuisance to anybody. If I knew I had terminal cancer I would make sure to die somewhere else, say in Fiji (laughs).

Of his scrapbook poems in French and English, he said: 'Strange! Although I am cheerful I find that most of the poems in this scrapbook of my favourite ones deal with love or with death.'
On another occasion he came back to the subject :
'When I die, I would like to die abroad.'
'Why abroad?' I asked.

'Because all Chairmen of Tatas have died abroad.'

'But that is no reason why you should.'

'I would like to die abroad, so I am no bother to people (here),' he said softly.

In this JRD had his way. His last illness was in a Geneva hospital. When visitors came to the hospital, he was embarrassed that they had taken the trouble to make the journey to see him. The person who visited him every alternate day there and at the same time carried on his responsibilities in Tata Zug near Zurich was Farokh Kavarana. On one of his visits, JRD looked at him and said: 'You are always there.'

● ● ●

BEYOND DEATH

One day I asked him if he could translate a French poem or two from his scrapbook. Without opening the book, he translated Baudelaire's 'O Morte' (O Death).

JRD : 'Captain, Captain (of the ship) to go, go, let's go, this country bores us.' What he means is life bores him . . . . And in the end he says, 'This fire burns me, burns me. Let me go, let me plunge into the abyss. Hell or heaven does not matter, but to find something new.' *Pour trouver du nouveau.* He only wants a change, bored with this life.

I have tried to write poetry, but it is impossible. You can do the first two lines, that's all.

RML : But you can recite it very well. You have read 'Abide with Me' here once, and I thought you read it very well.

I was thinking there are two ways of looking at death and the hereafter —one where you're just looking to get out of the travails of this life and the other where you actually see the future as a place where you will rest in the arms of someone, a sense that God forgives you, God loves you in spite of everything . . . . Some of the poems in your poetry book, which you have written down, are influenced by the war poems of World War I and thereafter, where death was a great reality.

JRD : Yes, there is a poem I really like by the poet Alan Seegar, the American who came to fight for France in World War I and who had the premonition that he was going to die. It happened exactly as he had anticipated. Martial poems, the old historical poems of battle, do not appeal to me.

RML : There are one or two of your favourites that I would like you to read.

JRD : There are some that I know by heart, including one called 'The Nomad'. Do you know 'The Nomad'?

RML : Yes, you showed it to me.

JRD : 'Nomad' is my great favourite. In English, at least, I like this poem the best. Why? Because it is a sad poem, it expresses despair; despair in the sense that you don't know where to go.

He then went on to recite the poem by Henry Shore:

When our ancestors found that wheat
Was a good bread to eat
They settled in Jericho.
All of us are settled now,

But in our souls there is great woe:
We don't know where to go.

I am settled in a fine place
I own a house, I live in grace,
I have a patio.
But late at night when the winds lament,
and the garden shivers—my soul is rent :
I don't know where to go.

One day when I say goodbye
To life and wife, and lie and fly
Somewhere in a great flow,
I shall be free to roam again.
I'll try to find but try in vain
Where to go, where to go.

RML : Does it reflect something in your own self?

JRD : I don't know. Yes . . . perhaps, I don't know what's
going to happen after I die. My father was a reasonably
religious man, because he prayed, prayed everyday. I heard,
I saw him. He prayed the whole time I was in the air on my
first flight when I was a little boy. My father told my mother
that he believed there was nothing after death, that there
was no survival of what is called the soul, that death was
final. Now that to me always seemed a little contradictory
in a man who prayed to God and yet you might say it also
showed his humbleness that while he knew that there was
a God, he did not believe that he himself was important
enough for anything of him to remain after physical life
had passed. In that sense, I am not like my father. I believe
in ghosts. If people who have died have been seen or have
expressed themselves in any way after the fact, well that

means that it can't be that there is nothing at all after death. So I said, all right, if there is something that I can look forward to, what is it likely to be? I would love to come back, if possible, with knowledge, but I know you can't come back with knowledge. I am interested enough to say that as I find this world, this universe exciting, if there is any likelihood of life after death, I would be curious just to see what's happening after I have gone.

RML : There may still be a place for you.

JRD : I hope that I live another three, four or five years, but that is only a minute in history. So I am getting a little more anxious to know what is likely to happen.

RML : You know, when someone very dear to you goes, as happened with my father, on the fourth day we have a certain prayer, and Parsis believe that you cross the bridge between heaven and earth at that moment.

JRD : What do you do in between?

RML : I suppose you are travelling, the 'airline' is taking you somewhere. Anyway, I was a bit concerned about him as you would be when someone dear to you goes. I was his only son. Then (at the prayers) I had a clear sense almost like someone speaking :'Now he is in the hands of God'. And a tremendous peace descended on me, in the sense that I felt I had to give him up now. I understood that I didn't have to be concerned about him as I was during his lifetime when he was ill or he needed help. Whatever it was, I was so grateful for this experience. It was God's gift to tell me at that moment.

JRD : 'Now don't worry. He is with me. He is in my hands'— No, I don't think I have ever had this experience. I am not sure that I had this feeling about my mother. Maybe I was too young to think. Don't forget, in 1923 (when she died) I was only nineteen and I had not read much and I had not thought much about things. Does everybody go to heaven across the bridge?

RML : No, there may be another bridge taking them somewhere else. I don't know. But you are right, the bridge is from this to the next life and the prayers are said that morning mainly to facilitate the journey of the soul.

JRD : I think everybody believes that there is a soul or something like that.

RML : I believe that. You know the whole concept of heaven and hell was originally a Zoroastrian concept. From Zoroastrianism it went to Judaism, and from Judaism it came to Christianity.

JRD : I must now begin to read about religions. They have had such a tremendous effect on history and continue to in many cases, like the conflict in the Middle-East, in Israel. In fact, I'm amazed that people of such great intelligence should have such an unreasoning belief in presuming superiority of their religion over others.

● ● ●

ON GOD AND RELIGION

JRD : I am anti-clerical, not even anti-religion . . .

RML : You're not anti-God. You don't talk against God, you're not an atheist in that sense.

JRD : No, on the contrary I think there must be something.*
But rather ineffective. Because what I see happening cannot
be the wish of a God. But when you see what's happening
in the world, the suffering, the horrors that are inflicted on
people, all that we see around—if there is a God in the
Christian sense or in the Muslim sense or in any sense you'd
like to call it, why does He allow such evil?

RML : Did you feel some kind of presence of God during
your flights and so on, during your long periods in the air?

JRD : No. The only time I would have was when I was in
danger and then you are busy dealing with the danger.

He said this in 1988. In an earlier conversation, in 1980,
I had asked him:'How did flying in those small planes affect
you when you were alone in the plane, without radio,
without instruments and without ground aids? Did you
feel there was a Creator?'
    'The fact that you find yourself totally alone in the
immensity of space makes you very humble and makes you
see of what little consequence you are. And then you identify
God with the immensity of nature. These are the only times
when I felt totally alone and was conscious of that
loneliness.'**

● ● ●

---

* In September 1988, he told the editor of a student's magazine *Pasha* :
  'To me God is some benevolent force, for the good of the people and
  the good of everybody.'
** Quoted in my book, *Encounters with the Eminent.*

It was July 1992—six months after the publication of my biography of JRD. At the start of the conversation JRD mentioned once again what a beautiful title I had chosen for the book, *Beyond the Last Blue Mountain*.

'Where did you get it from?' he asked and again read aloud the poem which appears in very few anthologies of English verse :

*We are the Pilgrims, master; we should go
Always a little further: it may be
Beyond that last blue mountain barred with snow* . . .

'You didn't get it from a book of poems did you?' he enquired.

I replied that everyday I did some inspirational reading and it was in the course of this that I came across this verse.

'Why don't I have any inspirational books? When I want inspiration all I read is about Jamsetji Tata,' he said. The talk moved from inspirational reading to prayer. He said he couldn't pray except on the death of his friends, when he would ask God to receive the person.

'The night nurse of my wife tells me that prayer is praise. But if I praise God, I also think of the things that concern me—the wars that take place, the poverty, the suffering. What about all that? Why does He permit it? If I do pray, say, for a friend of mine—'Please benefit my friend Russi'— I put myself in God's position and ask, 'Who is this chap that I should listen to him.'

'Ah!' I said, 'You are placing yourself in God's position!' He laughed.

I then quoted from some of the Psalms to illustrate man's

relationship with God. 'Bless the Lord, O my soul, and all that is within me bless the Lord.' I told him how much the Psalms had inspired my writing and I told him about the Authorised Version of the Bible and the beauty of the English language of the Elizabethan period. He wanted to know what more he could read of that period.

I said, 'You do believe in God, so why do you question prayer?' I went on to say that prayer is communion with God. Words are just one way of praying, the other is to be silent. 'Have you not felt sometimes at least a sense of peace descend on you? You may be against organized religion, but you believe in God.'

'O yes,' he said. 'But then I ask, "Why is it He has allowed all this suffering"?' *

● ● ●

MEETING WITH FATHER BALAGUER

Former Principal of St. Xaviers' College, Bombay, and Head of Jesuit Education in India, Fr M.M. Balaguer, as President of the Eucharistic Congress was the main organizer of Pope Paul VI's visit to India in 1964. An outstanding Jesuit, he has spent the last twenty years of his life training priests and nuns of all orders of the Catholic Church. Born in Spain, Fr Balaguer came to India at a young age and the day after India became independent, he applied for Indian citizenship. He has served Indian education in various capacities. A tall and dignified figure, he is proud of his

---

* The question of prayer is discussed at greater length in the next section under the title 'Abide With Me'.

Indian citizenship. When asked once what this country could do for him after all he has done for generations of Indians, the prelate, now ninety-four, replied: 'All I ask for is six feet of Indian earth.'

In 1990, Fr Balaguer had come to Bombay for his ninetieth birthday celebrations and visited Bombay House, the Tata headquarters. JRD came out of his office and said he was proud to meet him. They began by exchanging notes on ageing.

JRD observed that 'with age some mental processes do fail'. To which Fr Balaguer replied, 'Retention of all facts is not expected of you. Judgement is expected.'

JRD replied, 'I suppose so. It improves with age.'

The talk turned to creativity and JRD said, 'I've been given credit for a lot that I do not deserve.' Fr Balaguer observed that he had done a good deal in his lifetime. JRD replied, 'Yes, but one is never satisfied.' He mentioned that the Guggenheim Award (given to outstanding aviators) that he got was nothing to do with creativity. He said, creatively speaking, where aviation was concerned, credit was deserved by Aero Postale, a small French airline which flew mail services after World War I with little planes. Despite limitations like low altitude capability, these planes flew through the mountain passes of the Andes. The saying in those days was: 'That mail may be lost but never delayed; passengers may be delayed but never lost.' Such was the commitment of those early pilots that they took this risk and there were, of course, some crashes. One little plane failed to turn up at the appointed time. Some days later two men with over-grown beards arrived with mail bags on their backs!

JRD added : 'The Award I'm most proud of is the Dadabhai Naoroji Award.' He then went on to speak about Dadabhai Naoroji and his contribution to the education of Indian women.'

'I'm enormously fond of children,' he said, 'I play with them (at this point he stretched out his hands) but I've never had children.'

JRD also noted that if prosperity comes it makes one more selfish.

They talked about God and JRD mentioned his dislike for organized religion. Fr Balaguer noted that the Communists had tried to suppress God and found that nothing can take the place of God. He spoke of his own experience of God's calling and of his vocation as a Jesuit.

JRD agreed that God was love but pointed out that organized religion had prompted wars, including the crusades. Fr Balaguer suggested that he ought to read more about religion and arrive at his own conclusions on the subject. JRD observed: 'At twenty-one should find out what religion will answer all one's needs. Otherwise you end up believing in nothing. To me religion is service—one must play one's role.'

In the course of the conversation, Fr Balaguer related how he had joined the Church at the age of fourteen and how his father had explained to him through a book what vows like chastity meant. I asked Fr Balaguer whether in his seventy-five years of Jesuit life the three vows—chastity, poverty and obedience—had ever bothered him.

'Not once,' said Fr Balaguer. There was a stunned silence. 'You are lucky,' I said softly. JRD sensitively added, 'Maybe because it was God's calling for you.'

JRD then talked of his belief in reincarnation. 'Because I can't believe that a man is born to live for a second of a lifetime. I hope to be reborn in this world.'

Fr Balaguer observed: 'You may not necessarily be here.' Somewhat shaken, JRD asked: 'You mean I will be in some other part of the universe?'

'Not necessarily,' said Fr Balaguer. 'God is without time and space.'

'Then where will I be?'
'We shall either be with God or not with God.'
'What is there then?'
'The next life.'

When JRD seemed dissatisfied at his lack of knowledge about these matters, Fr Balaguer was reassuring. He said: 'You haven't given it enough time.'

JRD believed that if there was no God there was 'too much that was inexplicable.' He related the story of a ghost he saw in Geneva. At the foot of the bed of a sister-in-law who was ill, he saw a vision of the monk who had spoken at the funeral service of her husband. The monk had just looked at the patient and shaken his head to indicate that her condition was critical. This prompted JRD to arrange with the Air India people to look after her when he left Geneva. Soon after, she passed away.

JRD said to Fr Balaguer, 'It is a good influence meeting you.'

Fr Balaguer thanked him for the time he had given (almost two hours) and then said, 'I'm grateful for what you did for Russi last year (sending me to America for medical treatment).'

JRD replied, 'Anybody would have done it.'

'Yes, but you did it at the right time.'

As always JRD asked his visitor if he had transport back home.

After the interview, Fr Balaguer and I walked down the corridor quietly. I remarked to Fr Balaguer : 'I hope that before he moves on he comes closer to the Creator.'

'Don't you think he has already?' was Fr Balaguer's rejoinder.

A couple of days later, when I called on JRD, he was still

intrigued by his meeting with Fr Balaguer.

'Think of it,' he told me. 'The fellow never looked at a woman in all his life!'

*Fast falls
the
Eventide*

IV

GLIMPSES INTO A CRUCIAL YEAR—1991

I strove with none, for none was worth my strife
Nature I lov'd, and next to nature, art.
I warm'd both hands before the fire of life
It sinks, and I am ready to depart.

Landor

Sketch by J. R. D. Tata

GLIMPSES INTO A CRUCIAL
YEAR—1991

Nineteen ninety-one was a turning point for JRD. That year his health started to give way. He underwent four angioplasty procedures in England and the USA within a period of three months. It was also the year he decided to step down from his last company chairmanship—that of Tata Sons, the parent company of the Tata Group. This section comprises some fragments of notes I kept during that period.

Friday, 4 January—got a phone message at night to say that JRD was ill in the office about 6.30 p.m. Dr Gool Contractor came on the scene and found he had almost lost his voice. Dr F.E. Udwadia was summoned from his rooms. He said it could have been a mild cerebral stroke. The next morning he went for his MRI and another heart test. Dr Udwadia advised him to go to hospital but he insisted on resting at home.

Saturday, 5 January—Even after the results of the MRI and heart test were explained to him he insisted on going to the Taj in the evening for a function. He had a flaming row with Gool who insisted that he should not go. It was not an important dinner engagement but a meal with an American couple that could have been had at any other time.

It was doubtful whether he would be able to inaugurate the Tata Central Archives on Monday, the 7th. In view of his health I rang him about the Archives launching he was to preside over on Monday morning. I had arranged the function. I told Gool, where I was concerned, his health was a priority and we could get someone else to preside. Gool was anxious to prevent him from going out on Saturday. I asked her if I could ring him. She encouraged me to do so.

I rang him at about 5 p.m. I said: 'Sir, how are you?' He was rather surprised that I knew about his illness and asked me how I had come to know. I would not tell him. 'I want you to know that you are more precious than the function on Monday and you should do what your doctors tell you.' He was touched and said: 'Nothing much is wrong, only my pressure had gone up'. I again came to the point of his heeding the doctors and reminded him of what Sir Homi Mody had said about him: 'Our Chairman is a very versatile man. He likes to be his own doctor and makes a very bad one at that.'

He said the Monday function was not a strain on him. What worried him was the Meeting of the Rotary Club on 23 January. He recalled on the phone (over which he could have long conversations) that when he first joined the Rotary in Bombay in the early thirties, they met in a small room. Now four Clubs were gathering to hear him at Hotel President. He related to me what happened when George Bernard Shaw was present at the Rotary. An agitated Rotarian had asked, 'Where is Rotary heading?' Bernard Shaw had replied: 'To lunch.' JRD's humour cheered me and I felt nothing much could go wrong on Monday with a man who could crack such jokes.

Sunday, 6 January—I hear that Dabeh came to lunch. She is suffering from Alzheimer's disease* and no nurse will stay with her at home because there are seven stray dogs she has adopted. Her condition is quite a concern to him. He has not always been most patient with her but now he has got to be.

Monday, 7 January—For the Tata Central Archives inauguration he came just in time. Knowing what he had gone through on Saturday and Sunday, I wondered how he would cope with the function. But when he rose to speak he carried himself with dignity and gave a very lucid introduction on Tata Archives and spoke of how, when the Tata Airlines, by then Air India, was nationalized and all the records were taken over by the Government in 1953, he had recognized the need for an Archives for Tatas. He was happy his long-standing wish was now being fulfilled.

Monday, 14 January—Raymond D'Souza (his secretary for twenty years), says the Chairman is worried about the Rotary speech on 23 January. To relieve him of pressure, the organizers asked JRD to have a question and answer session, but he insists on making a speech and in that process is adding to the strain he is under. Raymond tells me: 'The speech is working on him, rather than he on the speech. You know how he is. He does not dictate straight. He will dictate something and then he will try to get the perfect sentence and keep changing it. He will argue with himself as he dictates, "What am I saying it for?"'

Tuesday, 22 January—He sent a personal letter to me regarding my impending chemotherapy treatment. He did not understand why I had asked the American doctor for advice on the local doctor's therapy as he (the American

---

* She passed away nine months after JRD died.

doctor) would feel awkward to disagree. It would have been better if the American doctor was asked for the line of treatment. 'If necessary,' he concluded, 'we may send you back to New York. If my help is needed I shall give it freely, as you know.'

I have so far addressed him in my correspondence as 'Mr Tata', and in conversation as 'Sir'. In his letter of the twenty-first he wrote, 'My name is Jeh and not Mr Tata.'

Wednesday, 23 January—I was late in coming to office today. He had tried to get me on the phone. When we finally spoke he chided me for coming to the office, saying, 'So long as you are under some treatment you don't need to feel that you *have* to come to office.' He repeated the points in his letter and said: 'You know I sent you to America the last time and I will make arrangements to send you again.' I replied that perhaps I should take the first shot here and thereafter consider going abroad if a visit was necessary. He left the decision to me. Dr Gool Contractor had told me earlier that when he read my letter about the possibility of fresh treatment he exclaimed: 'Oh God! Keep this man going for some time. I need him.' Many people wish that *he* would keep going for some time.

In his lifetime many have been drawn to him for his affection and his concern for them, yet how few of us have acquired the great qualities we so admire and praise in him. Perhaps when he goes we will realize this distance and attempt to acquire some of those qualities we have loved in him—his graciousness, his care, his kindness, his precision, his manners and his desire to help all those who come across him.

When anyone departs Jeh is fond of quoting a French poet: 'When someone we love dies, a part of us dies with them'. Perhaps when he dies, a part of him will live with us.

Thursday, 24 January—The Rotary Speech went off well. It was a question and answer session after JRD had said a few introductory words. He added a light touch to it. To one question he replied : 'There is no limit to what I am supposed to know!' Mr S.P. Godrej wanted to ask a question on family planning and environment but it turned out to be a short speech. JRD replied in two words: 'I agree.' (Applause.)

Some pertinent points JRD made were: 'Why is there such continuous disagreement and dissension in India when other nations can work together and go ahead? If nobody is satisfied, there must be a reason. The reason is in the belief that you can run this country from the Centre, and the fate of the various States can be regulated and influenced by New Delhi. That is why there is this dissatisfaction and upsurge in various States all over the country. For example, our fine Constitution provided that all industries except the strategic ones listed in a Schedule were to be controlled by the States with a proviso that Parliament can add to the Central list. In forty-five years the Parliament has selected ninety-five to ninety-eight per cent of industries, including the making of tennis shoes and razor blades, in the Centre's purview. Furthermore there is interference in the election of State Chief Minister's by the All-India Party based in Delhi. In a large country with a large population, people must have the freedom to decide for themselves.'

In an answer to another question: 'We are an undisciplined lot. I am not sure we are even loyal .... We must find a way to talk .... I am proud to be an Indian. We are among the most intelligent people of the world.' When asked if women should be put in power, he replied: 'Men have made such a mess of this world, women cannot do worse.'

When asked about Tatas, he said that the reason for its success is the reputed honesty, the sense of fairness, and doing the right thing, never contrary to the interests of the country. 'One reason why we do well is that we are not interested in merely the profit. It matters to us what people think of us (Tatas). When I became Chairman in 1938, I saw the need to ensure efficiency and character and the need to have the best people available.'

As he was going out he greeted me warmly: 'I did not know you were here! Let's go together.' So I accompanied him in his car. On the way he enquired about the progress with my doctor in America. I said I was hoping to ring the doctor on Friday. He said, 'It would be advisable to fax him that you are ringing him on Friday so that he is prepared and studies your papers.' It was a valuable hint as the papers had reached the doctor only on Monday and today was Wednesday.

We were speaking about a person who had the integrity but lacked the ability to deal with people. He advised: 'Why don't you gently tell him about that?'

On another point he asked me to have a word with a colleague and thoughtfully added: 'If he is a bit difficult, come and speak to me quickly about it.'

He asked me how I was feeling. I said I functioned but I lacked the energy to do all I wanted. 'Don't worry. When the disease subsides you will get back your energy.' It was reassuring.

As it turned out, his advice, particularly about faxing the doctor before ringing him, was most useful and I realized that unlike most of us his world does not revolve round himself. He thinks about what others are doing and facing. He lives into their lives, that is why he bears his own burdens bravely.

● ● ●

Friday, 1 February—Eight days later I was at the Tata Memorial receiving treatment. After a morning shot of chemotherapy I was having rigor about 8 p.m. I was buried under blankets. An office colleague, Rustom Davierwala, kindly attending to me then, came running into the room. 'Dr Contractor is coming and Chairman is walking behind her.' Always correct, he stood outside my room while the doctor came in. Dr Contractor said to me, 'The Chairman would like to come in if you feel like receiving him.' She left the room and he slowly walked in. I stretched out my free arm to greet him. 'It makes all the difference having you here, Sir. Thank you for coming.'

'Don't thank me. I have just come to see a friend.' I later heard from Dr Contractor that she was dropping JRD home in his car and continuing her journey to the hospital. When JRD heard she was coming to see me he said: 'I also want to see Russi.' She warned him the traffic would be heavy and the journey might tire him. It was well past 7 p.m. by then. He braved the traffic of the peak hours after a long day in office.

It was through this spontaneous care and concern that JRD took Tatas beyond being just an industrial group and lifted it to the level of a family.

Some time later I mentioned to JRD that it was relationships that built a company, not board meetings. I observed that you see the love of God in the love of people who care for you (e.g. his visit to the Tata Memorial Hospital to meet me). He replied: 'If you were not in Tatas I suppose I would have still come because I am fond of you, but the fact that you are also a Tata man does, I suppose, make a difference.' I mentioned to him that Ratan had said he had learnt a lot from him (JRD) about how to stand by people.

He seemed delighted and asked: 'Did he really say so?' He felt his attempt to train his successor was yielding fruit.

Sunday, 17 February—Dabeh is now installed in two rooms at the Taj. She has already spent about a month at the Breach Candy Hospital. All she needs is medicine four times a day. She has nurses in attendance night and day. The Chairman took her out to lunch. The lunch took its own time. The food did not satisfy the Chairman (it is the wrong restaurant to go to as it only serves snacks). 'The burger was too tough,' said JRD. Somewhat worn out, he came home.

Just before 6 p.m. Dr Contractor got a call to say that Dabeh had come down to the entrance of the Taj and was insisting on going home to see her dogs. She was apparently creating quite a scene. Dr Contractor rushed there to dissuade her. It was a very difficult time and when Dr Contractor rang up JRD, he was so exhausted, he said, 'Let her do what she wants. We cannot do any more.' In any case, three hours later she was settled in her room by Dr Contractor and others.

Monday, 18 February—I saw JRD in connection with his book. He was his usual bright self again. He was very happy with the lunch he had had that afternoon with the French Consul and his wife and it cheered him no end when they told him how much they loved India, how they went around the country by car and train and what a warm welcome they were always assured of here, unlike France where they were sometimes treated rudely even in bars and restaurants.

Somehow the conversation drifted to Dabeh and he confided, 'You know, she is not at all well.' I said that I knew that and that it must be a very great burden on him. He replied: 'Well, yes and no.' He paused and added,

'Although I am a small man I have broad shoulders for my burdens. Yes, I sometimes feel strained but I always manage to laugh. If you can laugh at things then you can carry the burden, except when there is a threat to the survival of your wife or your friend.'

He had spoken earlier of his brother Darab: 'Dabeh is developing some of the traits of Darab. In hospital she did not believe anything was wrong with her. She threw away her medicine and her bottles. Now I don't argue with her at all.'

Dabeh kept coming up in the conversation as we talked about JRD's brothers Darab and Jamshed (Jimmy). I said to him that a friend had told me that he (JRD) expected both Darab and Jamshed to keep the same high standard of excellence he expected of himself. I implied it did not help them. He replied: 'Darab, yes, but Jimmy * exceeded my expectations and did so well.' He went on to talk about Darab. 'He was very intelligent, but he was weak and had no discipline. As a child he had a violent temper and went into rages. He would walk out of the house and cross the street.' When I mentioned that Dabeh was very fond of Darab, he said, 'Yes, but she did not quite realize how ill he was. Darab stayed with her before he died. Perhaps the doctors tried to keep Darab going and managed to do that for some time but the poor man was more miserable than before.' Slowly he added, 'I am beginning to think that when the Lord calls you back, it is time to go.' It was the first time he had spoken to me of God in such a human, friendly way. He continued, 'There was something about Darab which was very, very difficult.'

He seemed hurt as he talked about that period and I did not feel it was for me to press it at that time. It was obviously

---

* Jimmy was the youngest in the family. JRD was very fond of him. He died in an air crash at the age of twenty-one in 1936

a sad relationship in his life.

Monday, 25 February—I cleared quite a few detailed points on the manuscript of the biography. I showed him the contents and the first four parts of the book, two of them on aviation, and requested him to look through them and give me a note if he wished, but not to try correcting small details in which he would usually get stuck.

He agreed that now that he had decided to have his biography published, he would co-operate and do what I told him to. I said that I wanted to get at least the first volume out (that is all he had permitted me in his lifetime) as the second one would come later. Teasing me he said, 'You tell me how long you want me to live and I will.'

I showed him the poem of James Elroy Flecker 'Hassan' from which, I said, I was taking the title for my book, as it expressed JRD's character well. He read it aloud slowly:

We are the Pilgrims, master; we should go
Always a little further: it may be
Beyond that last blue mountain barred with snow
Across that angry or that glimmering sea . . .

We travel not for trafficking alone;
By hotter winds our fiery hearts are fanned;
For lust of knowing what should not be known,
We take the Golden Road to Samarkand.

'It is beautiful,' he said, and he rather liked the title I had chosen from it: *Beyond the Last Blue Mountain*. I told him I imagined him flying his little Pussmoth over the mountains of Iraq, seeking to get beyond the last blue mountain. I explained that that was how I saw him, always pressing ahead, even in his eighties.

The subject came to the question of modesty and how he had not sat on his people and tried to control them but had let them develop. He thought aloud, 'Anyone who is intelligent and is the head of an institution realizes that the only way to ensure that the organization attains its full potential is by giving its key people full opportunity and freedom. I don't think I did it only out of modesty. I honestly think you cannot get the best out of a man unless the man feels that he has the freedom to have his own way, even if it is not my way. If I had asserted myself I would have suppressed their originality. This I never did consciously.'

He continued: 'My modesty has been partly due to the mistakes I have made. I made a number of mistakes, especially in Air India, and exercised my judgement too much at times. I did not admit that I did wrong. For example, A.C. Guzder, the Chief Pilot, and Bobby Kooka beseiged me to buy a bigger four-engined plane for Air India (he was probably referring to the then domestic airline). I refused. I realized they were right but it was too big a risk to take. Wrong again when I refused the offer to let Air India operate the night service. I realized it was a splendid idea, but was worried about the minimum safety facilities. I was wrong in not going by my own thinking but was inspired by what happened in America.'*

I pressed him to say where else he could have gone wrong, and he said, after some thought, 'In a number of cases, perhaps in dealing with the union of Air India.'

• • • •

---

* For further particulars see the Chapter on Night Air Mail in *Beyond the Last Blue Mountain*.

March 1991—In February he had worked very hard on his forthcoming speech on 'Business Ethics'. On the last day of February he attended a function for the Golden Jubilee of the Tata Memorial Hospital. He spoke too long, he admitted. Next morning JRD had some chest pain before his flight to Calcutta (en route to Jamshedpur for the Founder's Day ceremonies on 3 March). He did not tell his doctor and went to the airport for his flight. After three days in Jamshedpur he had exhausted his tablets—Sorbitrate—and wanted some more. When an annoyed Dr Contractor asked why he had not reported the pain, he replied: 'You would not have allowed me to travel.' With some persuasion from the Bombay doctors he saw the doctor in Jamshedpur, but went at the same time through a gruelling programme, including a one-hour oration which he insisted on standing up to deliver. He did not go by the text of the Business Ethics speech he had worked on so hard. 'My feet are a bit wobbly,' he told Mrs Homai Bodhanvala.

On returning to Bombay Dr F.E. Udwadia was called in. The doctor wanted to check whether his blood had thickened and also wanted to try and make him rest. After much persuasion from his doctors he agreed to go to the Breach Candy Hospital for a check up and have his blood tested every few hours. He entered the hospital on Sunday, 10 March. Come Monday, 11 March, although no visitors were allowed, a group of his directors went to see him. Tempted as I was, I waited till Friday, 15 March, to call on him. As he was leaving hospital the next day, I knew he should be better. I found him dressed in a deep blue sleeping suit with white piping, short sleeves, and short pants. He seemed very cheerful for a patient.

Good-looking daughters of a friend of his were with him. First he warmly enquired after me. He told the young ladies about his new Trust which was to grow quite a lot 'with the sale proceeds of my flat at Sterling.'

'You know,' he elaborated, 'I bought it for five lakh rupees in the 1960s and I am getting almost four crore for it from the German Consulate. At first they thought the price was too much and said no and I replied: "I am sorry, this is the valued price." Later they came back and agreed to buy it.' Towards the end he said how if he had been a Muslim and thirty years younger, he could have married those two young ladies! At this remark one of them turned to me and said: 'Look what he has reduced us to in this age of women's liberation!'

He came home on Saturday, 16 March. Within forty-eight hours of his discharge he turned up at the office. A director rang up to say : 'We are glad, Sir, that you have come to office today.' 'Why? Aren't you glad when I come on other days?' he retorted.

Eight days later he stepped down from the Chairmanship of his last company, Tata Sons.

● ● ●

Friday, 5 April—JRD has to have angioplasty, the heart procedure to open his arteries. When JRD learnt that the cost to have it done at San Francisco would be between U.S. $ 20,000-35,000, depending on the number of vessels they would have to deal with, he told his local doctors that the cost of the operation was too high and that he wanted to have it in Bombay. The suggestion was shot down.

He visits his sister Dabeh almost every day at the Taj for about an hour and a half after office and leaves from there at about 9.15 p.m. His doctor is concerned. He drops off to sleep in the car and is hardly hungry for dinner. There were some occasions when he dozed off to sleep at the dinner table. He cannot quite accept that his sister has lost her memory and still argues with her at times. He is so exhausted these days that the other night he told the night sister who took him his medicine, 'Why do you give me all this medicine, let me just die in peace.' The strain of having an invalid wife for ten years and now a sister (who is the only surviving relative he has in Bombay) is an unbearable strain. For a man so full of life to say these words shows he may be reaching the end of his considerable endurance. I asked him why he sees his sister almost daily and he said that she asks for him.

In his eighties he has everything a man could want—wealth, recognition, affection, health, a fascinating job. And yet when the day is done and almost everybody has left Bombay House, he stays on in his office—6.00 p.m., 6.30, 6.45, 7.00. And when his secretaries suggest he might go home, he looks up and says: 'What have I got to go home to?'

After the two angioplasty procedures in California to open his arteries, he felt fit and travelled in America, consulted another heart specialist in London, returned to India and plunged into activities as before. In June he went to England for a meeting of Tata Limited, London, felt uneasy and rang up the Royal Brompton Hospital for his London cardiologist. The cardiologist was away but JRD spoke to another doctor about the recurrence of chest pain and asked if he could come the following day for consultation. 'You are coming tonight to be admitted to hospital,' he was told. They opened one artery that night. Dr Gool Contractor was flown in from Bombay. A couple of days later I was in London and I called at his hospital at about 11 a.m. He was to go in for his fourth angioplasty at 2 p.m. Well shaven, he was sitting up in bed with his eyes closed. When he opened his eyes, Gool took me in and said, 'Just say hello.' As I entered he said: 'I must warn you that I am in a nasty mood.' He was having a battle with the nurses. He wanted a drink of water which was being denied him because he was to be taken for the operation.

I saw him the day after the operation in the ICU from the outside. Gool said he had bleeding that night and his surgeon had rushed at 3 a.m. The worst seemed over but we kept our fingers crossed. It was on or about 25 June.

● ● ●

Friday, 26 July—Both of us are back in Bombay. Saw him three days before his birthday. He had come home after more than a month abroad. He looked much thinner and weaker and said he had lost ten to twelve pounds.

The Deputy Editor of an evening paper was around with a photographer to take some photographs for JRD's birthday and he was having a long session. It was difficult to make the two of them leave, more so the photographer who was having a field day. JRD kept talking till he was tired and his throat seemed hoarse. He told the journalist that there was much to be proud about as Indians and much to be ashamed of.

After the journalist went I told him that he seemed tired talking and I did not want to take much of his time. 'Talking does not tire me but arguments do, and long meetings when one must pay attention.'

The main purpose of my meeting him was to get him to see the text of the biography. He had read only the first five chapters and the one on Nehru and himself.

I pointed out that in the first five chapters his markings, in my view, were needless. He was sub-editing my writing as he did drafts of his own speeches. I told him about the urgency of bringing the book out quickly and said that he need only correct the factual errors. I handed over the fairly bulky manuscript to him.

I told him I had decided to speed up the conclusion of the biography after my visit to him at the Royal Brompton Hospital in London. 'I saw you just before your fourth angioplasty procedure and I said to myself that the book had to come out in your lifetime and I speeded up my work on it.'

'So, you don't expect me to live long?' he came back. I replied that was not the reason, but I thought it would mean something to him if the book came out during his lifetime.

Then with a charming smile he handed back the file to me and said: 'You have my approval.'

I wanted another appointment to choose the illustrations with him but he said it was not necessary. He had earlier told me about only one picture he would like to see in it— himself in a sailor suit at the age of about eight.

I inquired about his health. He replied: 'First tell me about yours and then I will tell you about mine.' So I told him.

He replied: 'I am pleased about your health but not about my own. I would like to get your advice as one who has had to face a medical problem and adjust to life, but above all as a friend.'

JRD had been out of hospital for only a month. He had been told that if the arteries functioned for sixty days they usually continued longer, otherwise bypass surgery or another angioplasty was necessary.

He was in a sober mood that day. He said that between late April and June he had had four angioplasty procedures on his arteries. Dr F.E. Udwadia had told him that if the arteries got blocked again he would have to undergo bypass surgery. The doctor had told him that a Bengali gentleman had had a bypass at the age of ninety-one at Breach Candy Hospital and had returned home in good health. From the way he talked I could sense that JRD was not keen on a bypass. He said he was wondering what to do if the arteries got blocked again, something that could happen in the next thirty days. Once that happened he would have very little time to think and a decision would have to be made now. I inquired how often an angioplasty procedure could be done. He replied that the world record was ten times but that was on a much, much younger man. Both the time and the decision were weighing on him.

He mentioned that in the course of the last angioplasty a month earlier, a stent had been inserted to keep the artery open. As I was neither a doctor nor a patient of heart disease, I was not the right one to consult. I advised him to write or telephone his London doctor for advice.

JRD said that the last time, within two months of the operation the arteries had got blocked again and he expected something similar to happen in a month or two. I said the last time he had not been disciplined, rushing around America within days of the procedure, and it need not happen this time if he was careful. As to other points of advice, I said he should leave the office at a reasonable hour—six o'clock every evening rather than seven or seven-thirty. 'There is nothing I have to do at home. I like to read here or talk to friends like you,' he explained. I said at home he could put his feet on the sofa and read. I related how I had advanced my hour of bedtime to ten from eleven and enjoyed better health. He said he went to bed at eleven or eleven thirty and slept well. He said, almost in horror, that now he came to office almost at 11.00 a.m. or 11.30. (Till the age of eighty-five he came in at 10 a.m.)

When we were nearing the end of our discussion I took him to see his portrait in the TISCO office made a couple of decades ago. The publisher of the biography had suggested it for the cover. He said: 'I remember. But I don't think it is good because it is not me.' So we went down to the third floor to see the portrait. He sat in a chair at a distance to view it and said, 'It is not me, I look aggressive. I was never aggressive. I was never aggressive.' When I pointed out he could be 'quite determined and strong-willed,' he said softly, 'Determined yes; but aggressive, never. This portrait makes me look aggressive. However, you are the author . . . .'

At my request he proposed for the cover of the biography a picture of his taken only a year or two earlier. After much thought, another photograph of him in his late sixties was selected as more appropriate for the biography as the book primarily covered the most active period of his life that saw many achievements. He saw it when published and thoroughly disapproved of the selection of the cover photograph. Time and again, he grumbled about the selection as sweetly as he could. The photo he had selected represented JRD as he looked in the late 1980s, the period covered by *this* book. In belated deference to his wishes I requested the publisher to put that photo on the back cover of this book.

V

THE LAST YEAR

December 1992 to November 1993

AYODHYA
RIOT RELIEF
'I AM AT PEACE INSIDE '
FEARLESS NADIA
KIRA
THE FINAL BLOW
'ABIDE WITH ME'
GOING BEYOND

THE LAST YEAR

The last year of JRD's life began with the demolition of the Babri Masjid in Ayodhya—and its deafening repercussions in the rest of the country—and ended in the quiet setting of a Geneva State Hospital.

AYODHYA

On the occasion of the Long Service Awards to members of the Sir Dorabji Tata Trust in December, one of the staff, S. R. Suratwala, asked JRD what he felt about the destruction of the mosque in Ayodhya. He replied : 'It will take a long time to digest and accept what has happened in Ayodhya. I hope it is the last time that there will be such a conflict about religion. What has happened has hurt not only the Muslims but also Hindus who are secularists. In the long term I hope that it won't change the future of India.' He thought that this would be the last time a religious conflict would divide the country.

He paused and added: 'I cannot understand how erecting a temple is more important than building a great literature

● ● ●

RIOT RELIEF

On 4 February 1993, he presided over a meeting of the Tata Relief Committee to assist in the rehabilitation of victims of the communal conflagration that took place in Bombay soon after the Ayodhya events. Tata companies and Trusts allocated over fifty lakh rupees for relief through the Tata Institute of Social Sciences and the College of Social Work (Nirmala Niketan). JRD took a keen interest at these meetings and his personal involvment meant a lot to the social workers in the field who were present.*

At the end of the meeting, as we were rising to leave, with a wave of his hand JRD said : 'Just a minute. It is all right our planning material aid to these people, but who is going to answer the hatred?' For a minute everyone was glued to their places, before thoughtfully trooping out.

● ● ●

---

* The Principal of Nirmala Niketan Dr (Ms) Hazel D'Lima wrote when JRD died : 'What we treasure most is the opportunity that our College had to work in collaboration with the Tata Trust, with Mr J.R.D. Tata as Chairperson, during the riots that shook Bombay in December 1992 and January 1993. It was an encounter we can never forget in what it revealed to us of his humanity, his sensitivity to details affecting people's lives, his breadth of vision and his organisational efficiency . . . .While we mourn his loss, we treasure his legacy not just to the Tata world but to every Indian. Everyone of us feels proud to claim him as 'ours', and to nurture in our lives the values that made him so great.'

On 18 March 1993, we were going to Bangalore together, he to preside over the meeting of the Court of the Indian Institute of Science and I to attend one of its Committee meetings. As we moved off in his cream-coloured Mercedes, I thought of his words to me when I began his biography: 'I had a very poor opinion of myself because my father deprived me of a formal education'. As we emerged onto Altamount Road, I said to him, 'You are humble and modest, Sir. The fact that you did not go to a University is a factor that may have made you so. It is a very important factor in your life. But suppose you had taken the seat reserved for you at Cambridge, suppose you were a Doctor of Engineering, would you have been as humble and modest as you are today?'

After a moment's thought JRD said : 'Even more so, I hope. I would have said to myself, 'All right, I am a Doctor of Engineering but then there are so many things I don't know. There would have been a difference of realization or approach.'

His car was stopped at the traffic lights at Peddar Road and he was getting impatient. 'I will talk to Pasricha (Traffic Chief) some day. Traffic lights should never be so long, not more than a minute or two.' I said: 'You are patient where big issues are involved, but impatient about small things.' Just then he saw that I was struggling to write his replies on a small piece of paper, as I wasn't prepared for this interview. 'Look, you don't even have a proper pad to write on. Give me my brief case.' He pulled out his pad with J.R.D. Tata inscribed on it.

He proceeded with his reply: 'In big things it is important to record or write down. Once you write things down it helps in the thinking process. In the important things of life one should make the effort to think; it is not enough to be impatient or angry.'

I said I was intrigued by the fact that he didn't really seem to be 'enthusiastic' about the economic liberalization taking place, though it was something he had fought for all his life.

He replied: 'I don't think I have contributed anything in economic matters except in ethics and values where I have my own views. An ethical life is part of an economic life.'

On economic policy, he said, he was advised by others, first by Dr John Matthai who was also the Finance Minister (he was a director of Tatas before and after his term in Government), and thereafter by Dr F.A. Mehta. By now the car had neared the main road of Worli where six days earlier several people were killed by one of the bombs that had ripped through Bombay. We passed the shell of a blasted building. He looked out of the window, 'I cannot understand this pointless expression of anger through violence.'

Again he was restless at the slow traffic. His driver, Peter, once told me that in the old days as soon as he sat down in the car he would say, 'Chalo, chalo,' and Peter did not have a moment to lose between his boss sitting in the car and his starting it. 'Why are you always in a hurry?' I enquired. He was momentarily taken aback. He tried to explain it.

He said that he appeared to be in a hurry but, 'I am at peace inside.' Over a decade earlier, when I had commented to him that he was always fiddling with something in the office, either his spectacles, his pencils or his pair of scissors, he had also said, 'But I am at peace inside.'

I asked him if he had to live his life all over again would he have done anything differently. To my surprise he touched on the time of the Quit India session of the Congress in 1942 when he was tempted to join the freedom movement by stepping down from his Chairmanship of Tatas. I had never realized that he had actually been in a dilemma.

He added: 'I am glad I did not succeed in the idea of joining the Congress or the freedom movement.' Had he done so, he meant, his life would have been totally different. I inquired if he had talked to anybody about his desire to leave Tatas for politics. He shook his head. 'I couldn't talk it over with my office colleagues because after 1938 (when he was elected Chairman) they would not have allowed me.'

●　●　●

FEARLESS NADIA

One day in July 1993, JRD rang and invited me to lunch with a British journalist. On the drive to the restaurant, as the car was cruising along Marine Drive, Gool began talking about a documentary on Nadia, the famous actress who was a patient of hers.

JRD : Who's Nadia?

GOOL : She was a great actress of the 1930s and 40s. She performed stunts too.

JRD grunted. To impress him, Gool said : 'Other actors have stunt artists to perform for them but Nadia performed her own stunts. Once she even put her head in the mouth of a lion!

JRD : The lion must have been terrified!

●　●　●

❧

One day, around 1989, I got a phone call from JRD's
secretary asking whether I would like to meet a lady who
was the oldest friend of the Chairman. A few minutes later,
after I had said I would like to meet her, the large wooden
door of my cabin opened and a diminutive lady walked in.
Her hair was white, her eyes bright, her handshake firm.
She was eighty-nine years old—five years older than JRD.
Polish in origin, she had lived in the same town as Rasputin
and remembered the notorious figure walking on a footpath
opposite her home. A girl of eighteen when the revolution
came, she boarded a cattle wagon on a Siberian train to go
on the longest train journey in the world, towards
Vladivostock. The train stopped every few miles and finally
she got off near a border town on the Mongolian border.
After many adventures she arrived in Bombay in the early
thirties as the wife of the Consul for Poland, which was
when she first met JRD and his wife.

During World War II she did valiant work for Polish
refugees and was instrumental in JRD and Thelly adopting
two Polish children. The life of one of them, said Kira, was
saved by the love and motherly care of Thelly. After her
husband died, she was in a difficult situation financially
and JRD helped her set up a business. Interested in the
Montessori movement, she pioneered the making of
Montessori toys in India and remains one of the very few
people whose products are approved by the International
Montessori movement.

When she walked into my room she talked about her plans
to start a Montessori Research and Training Centre in
Hyderabad. I wondered whether time would permit her to
see through even the first phase of the project, but a day came
in July 1993 when JRD and I flew together to Hyderabad for

the inauguration of the first building. The car journey to the
inauguration was a terrible strain. The Contessa we were
travelling in was noisy and both Kira and JRD in the back
seat were hard of hearing. Kira talked in whispers (as deaf
people tend to do) and JRD got quite irritated, because he
could not hear her. I had to relay every word from Kira to
JRD in the midst of the rattling of the car. When we eventually
arrived at the venue, we discovered that everything was
beautifully organized, except for the fact that the Minister for
Education in Hyderabad, Mr P.V. Ranga Rao (son of Prime
Minister Narasimha Rao) arrived forty minutes after 11 a.m.,
the time of the inauguration. JRD was kept waiting. Knowing
JRD's concern for punctuality I thought he would be very
upset, but he kept his cool and was gracious to the Minister.
Needless to say, after the inauguration was over, JRD and I
were both exhausted. Kira was not!

Very confident of her health, she had once told JRD, 'Jeh,
my doctor says my heart is stronger than yours and my
blood pressure is better than yours.' JRD had looked at her
and replied, 'Kira, you are indestructible. The only way we
can get rid of you is to shoot you.'

The following day he met the Montessori people at a Trust
meeting and after that he met a somewhat unusual
politician.

Vasant Nageshwar Rao, former Home Minister of
Andhra Pradesh, called on JRD. He mentioned to JRD that
after reading my book, *In Search of Leadership* (New Delhi,
1986), on leadership which focussed on moral issues in the
lives of great men, he had decided to order his election
campaign on the basis of honesty—'Even if I don't succeed
in getting elected.'

'Why do you say you may not succeed? A man known
to be an honest man, and not out to use his position, has

tremendous scope to help people. People will respond to such a politician.'

'Use your position to inspire people,' he emphasized. In some ways he was asking this gentleman to do in politics what he himself had tried to do in business—inspiring people.

Normally film and sports stars are harried by autograph hunters, but the appeal of JRD was easy to see from the manner in which young and old approached him wherever he went. On the last flight from Hyderabad to Bombay, one smart character requested JRD's signature on his boarding card because JRD was the founder of civil aviation. I hadn't the good sense to get JRD's autograph on his own boarding card which I was carrying, but at least I preserved it. It turned out to be his last domestic flight.

● ● ●

THE FINAL BLOW

A couple of days after the Hyderabad visit, I heard that he had not come to office because he was not well and was suffering spells of giddiness. Friends were told he had vertigo. Some months later, Dr F.E. Udwadia told me that JRD probably had had a mild heart attack. He spent 29 July, his eighty-ninth birthday, at home, unwell. Bouquets of flowers poured in as usual at his home and office, most of them to be dispatched to hospitals.

On 11 August, at about noon, my secretary rushed into my

office and blurted out: 'Sir, something terrible has happened.'
Apparently, Dr Gool Contractor had been knocked down by
a car. She had been rushed to the hospital, but my secretary
said she had just heard that Dr Contractor was dead. My
thoughts went to JRD soon after I recovered from the shock,
for I knew she looked after him, his ailing wife and sister. That
fatal morning she had travelled in JRD's car, stepped out and
as she was crossing the road, she was knocked down. JRD's
driver had informed him about the accident.

The news that she had passed away reached Bombay
House first. It was a sensitive matter breaking the news to
JRD. His senior colleagues in Bombay House played for time.
Ratan Tata told JRD that Dr Contractor's condition was
critical and he was monitoring it. Not too long afterwards,
Ratan Tata along with J.J. Bhabha—with N.A. Palkhivala
following in his car—went to break the news to him. As
soon as they entered, he realized that they were bringing
him the sad news.

Dr Gool Contractor was sixty-one years old when she
died. JRD was a difficult patient and she was often very firm
with him. As she was strict, he used to call her sometimes—
and introduce her as—'Saddam Hussein'. She could be more
blunt with him than any of his other colleagues but he knew
she wanted the best for him and respected her. In the past,
JRD had weathered the deaths of many of those closest to
him: his parents, his sister Sylla, his brothers, and Dr Homi
Bhabha and Jean Bertolli in the Air-India crash on Mont
Blanc in 1966. When Leslie Sawhny had died in Breach
Candy hospital, he had put his head in his hands and said,
'Why? Why? Why him? What will I do without him.' In
those days, he was younger, stronger. Things were different
now. Gool Contractor had served him and his family with
exemplary devotion and run their home. His mind reeled
under the workings of fate that had robbed him of a physician

who he had thought would continue to look after his ailing wife and his sister if something were to happen to him.

That day something seemed to have died within him. His health was already deteriorating before the accident. He put on a brave front but behind it was the reality Mathew Arnold expressed so beautifully :

> *The foot less prompt to meet the morning dew,*
> *The heart less bounding at emotion new,*
> *And hope, once crushed, less quick to spring again.*

On 11 September, exactly a month after Gool's death, he spoke at a Memorial meeting for his late doctor without breaking down. He said he prayed for her 'peace of soul'.

William Barclay, who wrote extensively on religious affairs, had once remarked, 'Prayer is not flight; prayer is power. Prayer does not deliver a man from some terrible situation; prayer enables a man to face and to master a situation'.

JRD's prayers after Dr Contractor's death enabled him to face the situation. But, alas, not to master it. Perhaps a year or two earlier he could have also mastered the situation.

● ● ●

'ABIDE WITH ME'

This was the last major interview with JRD on 24 September, 1993. A fortnight later he left for Geneva—never to return.

There were two major condolence meetings for Dr Gool

Contractor. One within ten days of her death, organized by
her friends, with Fr Joe Pereira leading the service, the other
at Bombay House. At the condolence meeting at Bombay
House JRD spoke about how he did not usually pray but
that when he heard she had had an accident, he had begun
to pray. JRD also said that since then he had prayed for her
daily, hoping that God would give her soul peace.

I began the interview by saying how struck I was by his
speech a few days earlier. He brushed it aside. 'I say, I need
your help and Father Joe Pereira's on this matter of prayer
and I would also like you to arrange for me to meet Father
Joe Pereira.' Father Pereira and I had spoken together at
the first condolence meeting. He referred to the hymn 'Abide
With Me' * which was sung on that occasion. 'Whatever
you call it, hymn, or poem, it was Gandhi's favourite hymn
and also mine.' Then he added: 'But who am I to ask God
to abide with me?'

He seemed quite agitated about this and a good part of
our interview revolved around the subject. 'God has to look
after eight hundred million people in this country and six
billion in the world, how can I expect him to abide with
me?' He paused. 'What is the exact meaning of abide?'

I replied: 'To stay.'

'I could not find that, it is not even translatable (meaning,
into French).' He rang the bell and asked for his bulky
brown Random House Dictionary which only his peon
could lift. He looked up the meaning and read, 'Remain,
stay'. He said rather forcefully : 'Who am I to ask God to
stay with me. God hardly notices me.'

I replied: 'It depends on your understanding of God. If
God is your friend, would you not ask a friend to stay with

---

* As so much of this interview centres round 'Abide with me', I have
  included it in Appendix III.

you if you needed him? If I needed you would I not say: "Would you stay with me just now?"'

I quoted lines which I thought were from the Psalms:*

He walks with me,
He talks with me,
He tells me I am his own.

He paused, visibly moved by the verse. 'It is beautiful,' he said. And then added, 'But "Walk with me"? I think it is damn cheeky to say that. He has so much to do, why should he bother about me?'

We talked about prayer and I said it depended on one's relationship with God. I mentioned that I had found I could hardly pray for a couple of minutes without distraction and I had therefore asked Fr Balaguer how people like Catholic priests and nuns could pray for hours on end. He had asked me, 'What is your conception of prayer?'

'Prayer,' Fr Balaguer had said, 'is communion with God. You speak to him and he speaks to you as you would to a friend. That is one kind of prayer.'

Fr Balaguer had then explained that there were two other kinds of prayer. The second type was where we spoke to God but did not wait to listen and a third was the highest form of prayer where you didn't speak to God but you felt close to God, exchanging your thoughts with him without utterance, like two lovers sitting quietly on a beach who need not talk but know what the other is thinking.

I enquired of JRD, 'What is your concept of God?' He

---

* I later discovered the lines were from a hymn/song by C. Austin Miles. The chorus verse is: 'And he walks with me, and he talks with me/ And he tells me I am his own;/ And the joy we share as we tarry there/ None other has ever known.'

replied: 'I mainly thank him for being there not for what he
is but for being there at all. Then I manage to ask for
something. Gool died, give her peace, and when I die allow
me to meet her. I pray to God for her as for one who served
the world. What have I done for the world?'

He thought a bit more, and said: 'We were both like
drops in the ocean. He has over-helped me. Given this, it is
cheeky to say "Abide With Me".'

'Could you not,' I asked, 'look upon God as a friend?
The hymn says, "In life, in death, abide with me". If he is a
friend in life he will be a friend in death.'

'But if all my life, almost a hundred years now, I have
thought of him as too busy looking after the world, how
can he have the time to look after a useless person like me?'

'You have put the Creator within your limits of time and
space.'

To illustrate God's unbounded power, I added, 'They say
that there are billions of galaxies in space and more are
under creation all the time.'

I returned to the question of looking upon God not only
as a friend but as a father. The only prayer Jesus taught
began with the words, 'Our Father'. I then related to him a
story I had recently read from a Harvard speech by Jean
Vanier who started homes for the mentally disturbed and
retarded. The story was about the relationship that a
mentally retarded person had with God. One of them, Peter,
was a mongoloid. Every evening Vanier prayed along with
a couple of the handicapped. Peter was always present but
never said anything.

Then one day Jean Vanier asked him, 'Peter what do
you do when we pray?'

Peter solemnly said, 'I listen.'

'You listen? To whom?'

'I listen to Jesus.'

'And what does he tell you?'

Slowly Peter replied: 'He tells me that I am his beloved son'.

Here was a mongoloid, I said, who had very little in life but possessed a special relationship with God. JRD was listening intently. I ended by saying: 'Nevertheless, I am glad you do pray and talk to God.'

He smiled shyly, 'I have started praying only in the last year, and always at night. Of course, when someone like Gool died I did pray, and when my father and mother died I prayed for them. But never for myself. I say to myself, "What can God say to a person like me?"'

●　　●　　●

GOING BEYOND

He left India for Geneva on 9 October 1993. I saw him last on 1 October at a meeting of the Tata Relief Committee and later in his office. The Tata Relief Committee met within twelve hours of the devastating earthquake in Latur, Maharashtra. JRD was in the Board Room before some of us arrived. Even though in the last two or three years of his life the blood did not adequately flow into the brain, as a result of which his power of absorption was at times below par, on this occasion his mind was razor-sharp and he asked searching questions. A Telco representative stated how that morning his company had made arrangements to rush blood from Pune to the earthquake area and Tata Chemicals reported that it was flying another consignment of blood from Rajkot. The other Tata companies offered the

medicines that were needed and a third Tata company
offered a refrigerated container. A lady from Impact India
was involved. She informed us that the hospital train
'Lifeline Express', was two hundred miles from the scene
of the earthquake and would reach it within hours.

While we were debating these practical matters, once
again he was a step ahead of us. 'With so many houses
having crumbled and with precious belongings trapped in
the rubble,' he asked, 'would there not be cases of pilferage?
And how can they be prevented?' A former Cabinet
Secretary stated, 'Sir, they are in such a state of shock that
they will not even think of it for seven days.' The day after,
a front page item in *The Times of India* announced: 'Pilferage
at earthquake site.'

Fifteen minutes after the meeting, I had an appointment
with him. I was going away on a short leave the following
day as I was recovering from flu. He inquired how I was. I
replied, 'Not one hundred per cent.'

'Forget being hundred per cent,' he said. 'I have a terrible
back pain.' The important thing, he indicated, was to keep
going (as at eighty-nine he was soldiering on). After clearing
a few matters quickly I wished him the best for his time in
Geneva. That was the last time I saw him. Eight days later
he flew to Geneva, never to return to India.

As we've seen earlier, he always told me that he did not
want to die in this country, but would like to die abroad.
The point he was trying to make was that he did not want
to be 'a bother to people.' He was humble but not unaware
of his eminence and the 'trouble' his dying in India would
involve. Soon after his arrival in Geneva, two friends from
India went to meet him over a cup of tea. The conversation
centred round Tata Steel workers in Bihar giving one day's
salary for the earthquake victims of Maharashtra (officers

had given two days' salary). He was proud, very proud of the workers of the plant where almost seventy years earlier he had got his first work experience. He said he would write a letter of congratulations to the Union leader, V. Gopal. 'I'll write it with my own hand.' Alas, he lived to hear shortly after (on 15 October) that Gopal had been shot dead.

On 4 November, JRD was removed to the Geneva State Hospital with a very high fever and a urinary infection which was brought under control.

He knew he was nearing the end and he wanted to go. He told a friend in French, '*Comme c'est doux de mourir*' (How soft/gentle it is to die).

On 26 November, two of his doctors, Dr Dalal and Dr Udwadia from Bombay, met him.

Dr Udwadia asked, 'What is your major complaint, Jeh?'

'Don't you know, my dear Faroukh, it is age. After all I am eighty-nine.'

JRD had given up eating a couple of days earlier. 'Don't behave like a child,' remonstrated the doctor. 'You must eat.'

'Why do you want me to eat at my age? Why should I eat? Why should I not just shut my eyes and go.'

Simone Tata, then in Geneva, was with JRD in the hospital on 26 November. Following the visit of Dr Udwadia, JRD seemed somewhat brighter. Between spells of drowsiness and alertness, he suddenly opened his eyes and said in French to Mrs Tata, 'I am about to discover a new world. (Pause). It is going to be very interesting (pause) very interesting.' 'As he said it,' Simone Tata recalls, 'His eyes were sparkling as if he had seen a glimpse of that new world.' After that he went back to sleep. Three days later, in the early hours of the morning, he passed away.

● ● ●

Appendix I

JRD on Himself

From the Foreword to *Keynote*

W hen some of my colleagues in Tatas warned me
of their intention to publish a book of excerpts from the
speeches I had made over the past fifty years, I tried to
dissuade them from pursuing a project which I said would
induce a lot of kind people who had done me no harm to
pay for being bored. Not only was my advice brushed aside,
as an old man's usually is, but I was summarily called upon
to write a foreword.

Some of those who will have been misled into buying
the book will no doubt ask why I had to make all those dull
speeches and to expound in them unsolicited views and
advice on so many subjects on which I was not specially
qualified to speak. As they will have noticed, many of the
excerpts are not from speeches but from the Chairman's
annual statements to shareholders. I must confess I could
not resist taking advantage of the free forum, captive
audience and widespread newspaper coverage the
statements gave me to publicize my views, as head of the
largest industrial group in the country, on Government's
economic policies. I felt, in particular, that if my small voice
in the national economic debate could arouse public
opinion, it was my duty to use it to oppose the outdated
and sterile form of socialism which successive governments

insisted on inflicting on the country year after year despite all the contrary evidence and experience in India and elsewhere in the world.

Some of my speeches were made in answer to invitations to talk on subjects such as aviation, on which, like the one-eyed in the kingdom of the blind, I seemed to have established an exaggerated reputation for expertise and achievement. The fact, incidentally, that so many of the invitations were to talk only on aviation was good for my soul, deflating as it did any belief I might have had that I knew something also about business and industry.

One obvious weakness of the book from the reader's point of view is that, over the years, I said the same things over and over again. I couldn't avoid doing so as, until recently, my pleas for a change in economic policies were ignored. I hope they were at least recognized as being motivated only by a desperate desire to see a better life provided for our people than the miserable one in which, after thirty-five years of socialist planning and controls, deprivation, ignorance and hopelessness were still so heartrendingly reflected in the faces and eyes of so many of them.

I would have liked to end my foreword on this note, but I was instructed to draw upon my memory and recall important events or encounters which could be of interest even today. Unfortunately, I have little to offer partly because I didn't keep a diary, but also because most of what I could recall even with the help of a diary is either well known or could be of interest or amusement only to me or members of my intimate circle.

Some events were indeed important when they took place but mostly only to me. For instance, the occasion when, some forty years ago, in the excitement of the Quit India days, I attended a Congress public meeting at which fiery speeches by Jawaharlal Nehru and others led to some arrests. That meeting was a dramatic one for me. I was then torn between an urge to be personally involved in the freedom struggle and the realization that I could not do so meaningfully without deserting the heavy management responsibilities entrusted to me. I have never regretted my decision to stay out of politics which I rationalized to myself at the time by concluding that I could do more for the country in business and industry than in politics for which all my instincts, in any case, made me unfit. I had no doubt that freedom was on the way and that when it came Jawaharlal would lead the Government. 'Who knows,' I thought, 'I might one day have an opportunity to serve in more useful ways than going to jail today!'

I am often asked about outstanding people I have met in the course of my career, about my relations with them and my opinion of them. Those who made the greatest impact on me were, naturally, political figures, starting with Gandhiji, who led the freedom struggle.

Gandhiji, by far the greatest personality and, to this day, the most extraordinary human being I have ever met, inspired in me, as in most people, a mixture of awe, admiration and affection combined with some scepticism about his economic philosophy despite which one would follow or support him to the end, come what may. Perhaps the most unexpected and endearing trait I found in him was his almost childlike sense of fun to which he gave vent in a chuckle which he sometimes used deliberately to put one at ease in his presence. He was also, like Jawaharlal Nehru, the most considerate and courteous of men who would never leave a question or a letter, however unimportant, unanswered.

In his and my own youth, Jawaharlal was the heroic knight in armour who awakened in me some of the passion and fire that burned within him. While the love and loyalty

I had for him remained undimmed to the end, I soon found myself increasingly out of tune with him once he came to power. He knew that I disagreed with most of his economic and international policies, which perhaps explained the fact that our contacts, while always warm, became increasingly infrequent after he became Prime Minister and neither he nor Indira Gandhi ever found any need to consult me or to have me do anything for Government except letting me lead Air-India for twenty-five years after nationalization. My relations with both were wholly on a social plane, based on mutual friendship and affection.

Vallabhbhai Patel was the one with whom I felt most in tune and for whom I developed the greatest personal admiration and respect. While I was awed by his formidable political and administrative talents, the source of which was difficult to understand in a man of his background, one could not but be enormously impressed by the clarity of his mind and the simple good sense and logic with which he addressed and solved seemingly intractable problems.

While I usually came back from meeting Gandhiji elated and inspired but always a bit sceptical, and from talks with Jawaharlal fired with emotional zeal but often confused and unconvinced, meetings with Vallabhbhai were a joy from which I returned with renewed confidence in the future of our country. I have often thought if fate had decreed that he, instead of Jawaharlal, would be the younger of the two, India would have followed a very different path and would be in better economic shape than it is today. Vallabhbhai's stern and somewhat forbidding appearance concealed a warm and considerate personality which endeared him even to the tough British and Indian civil administrators he ruled over after Independence. On top of it, he had an unexpected sense of humour of which I was myself once a victim. On one occasion I will never

forget, having requested an appointment with the great
man, he asked me to join him in his morning walk to which
I was happy to agree, until I found that it was to be at 5
a.m., and that he had given the same appointment to three
others! As can be imagined, the four of us spent the next
hour mainly in pushing one another aside in order to get in
a few words of our own, only to be pushed aside in turn.
Vallabhbhai was visibly amused by our antics.

Of all the politicians I have known, Jayaprakash
Narayan was, in many ways, the least representative of
the breed, but one for whom I developed an unbounded
liking and admiration. I first heard about him when, during
World War II, he had gone underground in or near Bombay
and indulged in the delightful activity of toppling Tata
Electric high-voltage transmission towers in order to
interrupt power supply to Bombay. He and his men soon
discovered that sawing through the legs of a tower which
stood in a straight line with others merely made it sag
without breaking the electrical connection, while a tower
forming an angle with others, similarly attacked, obediently
collapsed on its side. Jayaprakash was betrayed to the police
by the Communist Party who, by then, had somersaulted
from being violent opponents of the war effort when Russia
joined Germany's attack on Poland and Western Europe,
into sturdy supporters when Hitler attacked Russia.

I personally met Jayaprakash only some years later in
connection with some labour problem at Jamshedpur and
was impressed by his transparent sincerity and gentle
reasonableness, unexpected in an ex-revolutionary activist.
It was, in fact, this unreasonable reasonableness, which I
believe, prevented him from being an effective political
leader and playing the powerful part he could have played
in Indian politics. He was too honest and too prone to see
the other side and to accept compromises and would never

be a party to the political shenanigans into which Indian politics increasingly sank in spite of Jawaharlal's effort to keep the political arena clean. Jayaprakash died a sad and disillusioned man whose friendship and regard I felt privileged to have earned.

My second longest and closest association with a political leader was, of course, with Indira Gandhi with whom my relationship was very similar to the one I had with her father. We were good friends socially but, as with Jawaharlal, I never was able to break through the fence which they both built around themselves. While I regretted the limitation in our relationship which deprived me of the chance to communicate freely with them on matters of national interest about which I felt I had something worthwhile to say, it helped to maintain, unspoilt, a friendship which persisted till the end.

As I said after her death in a small contribution to a book about her, there were two distinct Indira Gandhis— the shrewd and all-powerful politician-statesman and the gracious, cultured human being for whom the expression 'civilized' in the best sense of the term was particularly apt. She was a very complex person whose character and deeds will fully emerge only when sufficient time has passed after her death for uninhibited reminiscences and biographies to be published about her.

Politicians were not the only distinguished people it was my good fortune to know and to be associated with. The most outstanding of the distinguished men I have known was, undoubtedly, Homi Bhabha. In addition to the unique intellectual gifts nature had bestowed on him, he was, in the mould of Jamsetji Tata, a visionary with the boldness, relentless energy and drive to convert his vision into reality. Homi was one of those who made me believe that some men in human history are born with the stamp of predestination on them which leads them to accomplishments beyond ordinary human capabilities. Some of them—and Homi, alas, was one—are also predestined to die young, an unconscious premonition of which drives them to superhuman effort to complete their task in the short time allowed to them.

It has been a source of great satisfaction to me that I was able to play a part, however small, in helping Homi Bhabha to launch a programme which led to his magnificent achievement in making India, in a mere two decades, virtually self-sufficient in nuclear science. Scientist, engineer, master-builder and administrator, steeped in the humanities, in art and music, Homi was a truly complete man.

An odd trait of his mental make-up, however, was his disdain for time which made him somewhat casual, at times, in his dealings with people. This seems to be a privilege attached to great mathematicians, including Einstein and Paul Painleve, for a time Prime Minister of France, who was once found sitting at the top of the stairs outside the door of his Paris apartment waiting for Mr Painleve to return as promised in a note pinned on it by himself when he had left a little while earlier!

One of Homi's distinctive traits was his ability like that of Gandhiji and Jamsetji Tata to create men, in contrast to others under whose leadership no one of outstanding merit ever seemed to emerge. I believe that the greatest contribution Homi made to India's development into the modern state it is fast becoming, lies in training and bringing out to their full capability a host of young scientists and relations in industry, industrial philanthropy, all of which I am glad to say have become widely recognized as the Tata industrial ethos.

I shall always be grateful to men like Homi Mody, Ardeshir Dalal, John Matthai, J.D. Choksi and others who have passed on, after serving and adorning the firm for many years, and to those happily still with us whom I need not mention by name, who brilliantly carry the burden today.

My colleagues responsible for this book have insisted that I present in this foreword a 'more intimate image of myself, my personality, of what makes me click, than can be drawn from my speeches.' What can I say about myself that isn't either well known or insignificant?

While I consider myself a reasonably nice and dependable fellow, unaddicted to drink or gambling, fond of children and animals—I am ready to plead guilty to a number of faults or weaknesses.

For instance, I have a nasty temper when provoked which, annoyingly, seems to have no effect on those at whom it is directed, least of all my wife. I suffer from an irresistible urge to correct not only my own drafts, letters or speeches, but also those of others, much to the distress of my long-suffering secretaries whom I must have driven up the wall many times and to whom I shall ever be grateful for their understanding and patience. My excuse for my correcting mania lies in my abiding love for the English language, so often profaned in our country, which makes me forever search for a better word or turn of phrase. I have corrected the draft of this foreword three times.

I confess to being excessively intolerant of slipshod work and irritatingly insistent on pursuing excellence even in tasks which hardly demand it.

I don't mind admitting also to a number of continuing love affairs: a lifelong one with languages, literature and poetry of France and England, which makes me wish that more of the little formal education I have had, had been in one of the rich and beautiful languages of our own country. Another, the happiest as well as the most demanding one, has been with flying; a third with sport, particularly with highspeed driving, and skiing in which I still happily court minor disaster every winter, alas, with diminishing skill and vigour.

Friends who tell me it is ridiculous and foolhardy for an octogenarian to ski, fly a plane or drive fast cars, do not understand the thrill and sense of self-fulfilment obtained from living a little dangerously. In fact, to me, the cruellest penalty of age is the relentless loss of physical ability and of opportunities to indulge in it!

Apart from these flaws in my character, there is little of interest that I could publicly divulge about my private life. I find it much more fun to leave undisturbed such illusion as may exist in the minds of some people about allegedly fascinating events in my life.

I now leave you, dear reader, with the option either to put away the book, or to turn the page and read on.

J.R.D. TATA
April 8, 1986

Appendix II

As His Biographer Saw Him

The author has often been asked how he viewed JRD as his biographer and what was his interaction like. This appendix gives his personal impressions not only as a biographer but also as co-author of his speeches and author of the bestselling The Creation of Wealth: The Tata Story

—Editor

I interacted with J.R.D. Tata on three books—*The Creation of Wealth: The Tata Story*; *Keynote*, a collection of his speeches; and *Beyond the Last Blue Mountain*.

In 1979, after four months of research and writing early chapters on Tatas for *The Creation of Wealth*, I asked to see him. He was correct but cool in the beginning.

'In what capacity are you writing it? As former editor of *Himmat Weekly*, looking at Tatas from the outside?'

'Yes, but who is interested in Tatas? Who is bothered about Tatas?'

He talked along these lines for some time. I could see my work of months crumbling if I did not have the cooperation of the man who symbolized Tatas to the world.

Finally, exasperated, I tapped the table firmly : 'Sir, the hand of history has woven the tapestry of Tatas and it is a story that has *got* to be told.'

He did not expect that firmness or that conviction. He visibly jerked himself up, eyed me with a questioning look, and enquired: 'All right, what can I do for you?'

I asked him for figures of Tata Sons holdings in major Tata companies. He called for a folder, unfolded a big sheet, and on his calculator worked out the percentages.

The next question was loaded: 'What holdings does the Tata family have in Tata Sons if eighty per cent goes to the Trusts?'

I thought I was rather smart. Even twenty per cent of a gold mine is not negligible.

'The family doesn't own much. I can't tell you the percentage. But an outside party, with no connection with the family, owns a good deal. I'll ask Tata Sons to send you the figures.'

The figures came the next day. When I saw them I was humbled. The Tata family owned 1.53 per cent, the outside party owned 17.45 per cent, and the balance of about one per cent was divided between Tata directors.

I was struck by the openness of the man. I later found out that he questioned not only me but other people to test their conviction and not necessarily because he disagreed with them.

A few more interviews followed but contact with him was still limited in 1979-80. When *The Creation of Wealth* was published, he read every word of Part I and even marked very minor points and sent me the copy.

In 1982, on the eve of his Golden Jubilee Karachi-Bombay flight, he was unwell and refused all press interviews. He did, however, grant me an interview, probably because he thought well of *The Creation of Wealth*.

A couple of years later I started compiling his speeches and editing them. His senior advisor, S.A. Sabavala, had first mooted the idea and we worked on the book together. After eighteen months of work we gave JRD the manuscript on a Friday. The following Monday we were waiting in his office when he arrived. He opened one of his two weekend brief-cases and banged the manuscript on his table. 'See how much I've got to read? Papers, papers, papers. My whole weekend went in that. And who is going to read these boring speeches anyway?'

Even Sharoukh Sabavala was taken aback by JRD's reaction and we silently slipped out of his room. It was the wrong weekend to have loaded it on him. He was still the Chairman of major companies.

Some months later, Mr Sabavala was en route to the USA and his path crossed JRD's in London. This time he gave JRD an ultimatum. 'On your return to India either you co-operate with Russi Lala on your speeches or we will go ahead and publish them in any case.'

It worked. On his return we met. He made a few valuable suggestions. Then he sat down to write a charming foreword to the book.

One day he asked me to sit with him as he read aloud the draft of the foreword. He would say of a para on page two: 'It doesn't fit here.' Then, on page seven, he would say: 'It is better here.' The para would fit perfectly. I was amazed at the skill and thoroughness of his editing.

He began the foreword with the words : 'When some of my colleagues in Tatas warned me of their intention to publish a book of excerpts from the speeches I had made over the past fifty years, I tried to dissuade them from pursuing a project which I said would induce a lot of kind people who had done me no harm to pay for being bored. Not only was my advice brushed aside, as an old man's usually is, but I was summarily called upon to write a foreword.'

When the book came out he was pleased with its production, personally supervised by the Managing Director of Tata Press, Xerxes Desai.

There was a glittering function to launch it in Delhi at the Taj on his eighty-second birthday. The then Vice-President, R. Venkataraman, presided. L.K. Jha, ICS, spoke warmly of JRD. He recalled what had happened once when he was travelling with JRD on Air India. JRD left his seat. After some time L.K. Jha wondered where he had gone. JRD turned up after an inordinately long time. When asked what had happened, he replied : 'Oh, I went to see if the toilets are clean, and that everything is as it should be.'

'But what took you so long?' Jha enquired. JRD replied : 'The toilet rolls were not placed properly.' It turned out that the father of Indian civil aviation had gone to each of the several toilets in the Boeing and personally corrected whatever was wrong. As Jha recalled, it was this kind of attention to detail and concern for service that made Air-India, under JRD's stewardship, one of the premier commercial airlines in the world.

L.K. Jha concluded his speech by saying that JRD was catching the last plane that evening to be in Bombay before midnight so that he could be with his wife Thelly on his birthday.

After the function many came asking him to inscribe their copies of *Keynote*. He inscribed mine with the words :

To Russi Lala, with warm and sincere thanks for taking so much trouble in the preparation of this book. The only thing in it unworthy of its beauty being its contents.

Jeh Tata
29th July 1986

When *Keynote* finally came out, he was rather pleased at the attention it got. He received several requests for autographed copies and scores of appreciative letters, barring one. An up-country reader, a principal of a college, called his speeches 'boring'. Delighted, he sent me the letter with his noting: 'At last, a man of judgement!'

In 1983, when I first mooted the possibility of a biography he said casually, 'Can it not wait till I step down from my chairmanship of companies?' He gave me a couple of interviews and then would not readily give me an appointment for an interview. I was told by his senior colleagues that he wanted nothing published in his lifetime. I did not press him.

One day in 1985, his colleague and confidante, Jamshed Bhabha, took me along to his room. He tried to tell JRD how important it was that his life be recorded and written and that I was the man to do it. Again, JRD was difficult. Mr Bhabha attempted to press him on the point. JRD resisted. The more Mr Bhabha pressed him, the more obdurate he got. 'I don't want my biography to be written in my lifetime.' JRD rang Mr Sabavala and said: 'Sharoukh, Jamshed Bhabha and Russi Lala (actually I was silent) are harassing me to have my biography written. Are you free to come over?'

Three minutes later, the door opened. As he walked in, S.A. Sabavala said, 'And who is harassing my good friend?' There was a temporary lull. Then the battle started again. This time Mr Bhabha was exasperated. 'Jeh,' he said, 'If you don't let Russi Lala at least record your memories, it is dereliction of your duty.'

That got him. He sat up in the chair, squared his shoulders and said sharply, 'Jamshed, are you *deliberately* trying to annoy me?

Sabavala deflated the crisis. 'Jeh,' he said softly, 'we want to know, for example, about those early years. What was Jamshedpur like when you first landed?'

The frown relaxed. His mind travelled sixty years down memory lane. He recollected Dinshi Gandhy with whom he stayed. 'I haven't met anybody who could swear like him,' he started with a smile. 'On payday he would line up all his servants. He would walk down the line and as he handed out the salary he would use the choicest Parsi epithets, "You so and so".'

Relaxed by now, he agreed that his life be only *recorded* by me on condition that nothing be published in his lifetime. I agreed. Had these two friends, Mr Bhabha and Mr Sabavala, not helped, the record of his life would certainly not have been complete. Archives can only take a biographer that far. Only he and his sister (Dabeh) could give the story of his early years.

Mr Sabavala then asked, 'What is a good time for Russi to meet you?'

'When I come to office on Monday mornings,' he replied, 'I have cleared all papers and have no work for the first hour. In fact, I am wondering if I should learn Hindustani in that hour. Russi Lala can come 10 a.m. next Monday.'

Here was a man in his early eighties absolutely on the top of the job who cleared all his papers and wanted to study more. 'How many of us, with lesser responsibilities can say that?' I asked myself. In practice Monday mornings were not always possible because of other pressures and appointments. Most of the interviews were finally taped between 1987 and 1989. I found he was more relaxed at his home on Saturday or Sunday mornings and I preferred to see him there.

In the months to follow, JRD would often say, 'I don't want my life to be written, but if anybody is to write it, I would rather have you write it than anyone else.' Later, I arranged with him, through an exchange of letters, that I would have 'complete freedom in the text of the book,' words which he himself originally used when we were discussing the terms. To ensure complete freedom I kept the book clear of any commissioning by a Tata company.

JRD was eighty-three when the interviews started in right earnest. When your subject is that old, it is a race with time. I was not too worried about the later period of his life which was at least recorded in letters (over 25,000) and in the recollection of living personalities. What I was terribly keen on was to have some idea of his early years—something that only he could tell me about. JRD's surviving sister Robadeh (Dabeh) added to the details of JRD's parents. I am grateful to her.

Once the early years were covered I breathed a sigh of relief. I moved next to the years when he was absorbed with aviation, his distinctive contribution to India. While writing on his early years I had occasion to go to America and broke journey in Paris. I wanted to see the place where he was born and where his family members were buried. He was born in a magnificent apartment building near the Opera which incidentally now houses Air-India's offices in Paris. The place where his parents are buried, and where JRD was finally laid to rest, is a grand place expansive with trees and beautifully fashioned mausoleums, some with Greek motifs. The R.D. Tata family mausoleum is a wide one with torches engraved at either end, signifying the Zoroastrian symbol of fire. In that cemetery is buried Alfred de Musset, one of JRD's favourite poets (who wrote the words of *La Marseillaise*). Lying there is Chopin, his fingers stilled, his music resounding round the world. On a Saturday morning I saw young couples, some with flowers to place at the tombs of their dear ones. Surprisingly, Chopin's tomb had two or three floral offerings—a rare tribute two centuries after his death. It is among these poets that JRD, a lover of French and English poetry, rests now.

Although I was in a race with time to get his recollections and had prepared questions for each interview, I never rushed him. Sometimes he would digress, either recollecting or talking of whatever mattered to him at the moment. I had to be patient and let him go at his own pace. He was too big and spacious a person for me to fit into my work-programme. This kind of free-wheeling ultimately forged a relationship where it is fair to say that we both began to enjoy each other's company. We often exchanged jokes or a poem. He had an incredible memory for long poems, especially in French, many of which he recited and translated for my benefit. One of his favourite English poems was Alan Seeger's—'I have a rendezvous with death/ At some disputed barricade . . .'

JRD wanted his own rendezvous with death abroad and his wish was fulfilled.

Although we became good friends it was clear that he still did not want his biography published in his lifetime. When I once asked to see him at his home on a Sunday in 1990, he said to me: 'You are a persistent fellow. I feel sorry for you, because for all the trouble you are getting nothing. You know nothing is going to be published in my lifetime and I am not going to oblige you by going sooner. Why are you wasting your time? What are you getting out of it?'

Until the book was published there was to be no royalty for me. That Sunday morning I proposed to him that he gave me permission to publish his biography in two parts, the first volume upto the death of Jawaharlal Nehru to be published in his lifetime. Most personalities of that period were no more, I said to strengthen my case, and I suggested that first part would cover the period until Nehru died because it 'was the end of an era for India'. 'And for me too,' he came back quickly. JRD agreed to that volume of this biography being published in his lifetime.

Six months later, on 25 March 1991, he stepped down as Chairman of Tata Sons. On 5 April I met him. He was shortly going abroad for his first angioplasty procedure. This time it was he who said: 'Now that I have stepped down from Tata Sons, my last company chairmanship, when are you bringing out my biography—in one or two volumes, *whatever you want*.' It was a relief to get the green light. True to his conviction of 1983, the book had to wait till he 'stepped down from the chairmanship of companies.'

Come June that year and he was at the Royal Brompton Hospital. Within three months he was going in for his fourth angioplasty procedure and he was already eighty-seven. I realized that not only was time short for him but also for the completion of my book. I was working on the book alongside my pressing office work. I had myself just come out of hospital in London. I visited him in hospital. As I looked at his face through that little window outside his room, the thought flashed across my mind: 'I will never be able to forgive myself if I don't complete my book in his lifetime.' The next three months I overstretched myself. The book was completed, though at some cost to my health.

As luck would have it, the publishers released it on the eve of Republic Day, the day he was awarded the Bharat Ratna.

● ● ●

Appendix III

Abide With Me

Abide with me; fast falls the eventide:
The darkness deepens; Lord, with me abide!
When other helpers fail, and comforts flee,
Help of the helpless, O abide with me.

Swift to its close ebbs out life's little day;
Earth's joys grow dim, its glories pass away;
Change and decay in all around I see:
O thou who changest not, abide with me.

I need thy presence every passing hour;
What but thy grace can foil the tempter's power?
Who like thyself my guide and stay can be?
Through cloud and sunshine, O abide with me.

I fear no foe with thee at hand to bless;

Ills have no weight, and tears no bitterness.
Where is death's sting? Where, grave, thy victory?
I triumph still, if thou abide with me.

Hold thou thy cross before my closing eyes;
Shine through the gloom, and point me to the skies:
Heaven's morning breaks, and earth's vain shadows flee;
In life, in death, O Lord, abide with me!

H.F. Lyte (1798–1847)

INDEX